ISBN 978-1-331-75196-0
PIBN 10230095

SIX MONTHS IN A CONVENT,

OR, THE NARRATIVE OF

REBECCA THERESA REED,

WHO WAS UNDER THE INFLUENCE OF THE ROMAN CATHOLICS ABOUT TWO YEARS, AND AN INMATE OF THE URSULINE CONVENT

ON

Mount Benedict, Charlestown, Mass.,

NEARLY SIX MONTHS, IN THE YEARS 1831-2.

WITH SOME PRELIMINARY SUGGESTIONS BY THE COMMITTEE OF PUBLICATION.

BOSTON:

RUSSELL, ODIORNE & METCALF;

NEW-YORK, LEAVITT, LORD AND CO.; PHILADELPHIA, WILLIAM MARSHALL AND CO.; CINCINNATI, C. P. BARNES; AND ALL THE PRINCIPAL BOOKSELLERS IN THE U. STATES.

1835.

Stereotyped by Shepard, Oliver & Co.

PRELIMINARY SUGGESTIONS

FOR CANDID READERS.

It is related in the history of the Reformation, that about the middle of the year 1520, Martin Luther published in his native language a little treatise, in which he addressed the emperor and German nobility on the necessity of a reformation in the church. Some friends of Luther, however, there were, who were startled at the boldness of the publication, and CONSIDERED IT AS THE SIGNAL FOR WAR; but the more thinking and judicious part of mankind looked on this measure as the wisest step which, even in a merely worldly and prudential light, could possibly have been taken to render contemptible and abortive the expected fulmination of the Roman court.

This little treatise was the origin of that immense movement in public sentiment, the Protestant reform in the church. No sooner was it known, than Leo X. issued that famous damnatory bull against Luther, which in the event proved so fatal to the established hierarchy. The writings of Luther, though at that period they were of a mild and persuasive character, were condemned as heretical, scandalous, and offensive to pious ears; all persons were forbidden to read them upon pain of excommunication; such as had any in their custody were commanded to burn them; and he himself, if he did not in sixty days send or bring his retraction to Rome, was pronounced an obstinate heretic, was excommunicated, and delivered unto Satan for the destruction of his flesh.

We do not propose to institute a grave comparison between Luther's little treatise in the sixteenth century and the Narrative of a six months' residence in a Convent in the nineteenth century, but there are some points of resemblance in the treatment of the two cases that are not altogether unapt.

In August, 1831, a young lady, then eighteen years of age, a daughter of one of our fellow-citizens residing in Charlestown, became an inmate of the Community of Nuns established at Mount Benedict in that town, and voluntarily submitted for some time to a course of study and discipline designed to prepare her to become a teacher in the Convent, and a religious recluse for life of the Ursuline order. After a residence of about six months, she became dissatisfied with the religious profession she had embraced, and desired to return to her friends, against whose wishes she had renounced the Protestant for the Catholic faith. Having sufficient reason for believing that her return to the world would be opposed, and having no means of communicating with her friends, she made her escape, without the knowledge of the Superior of the Convent, and was restored to her former friends and her former religion. Soon after leaving the Convent, she became a member of Christ Church in Boston, of the Episcopal order, of which Rev. Mr. Croswell was rector. Her departure from the Convent happened in February, 1832, and in August, 1834, two years and five months having elapsed, the Ursuline Convent was burnt to the ground by a lawless mob. Since the commission of this outrage, a most cruel attempt has been made by the friends of the Convent to connect it with the young lady who escaped from the Nunnery in 1832, and who, from that period up to the time of the riot in Charlestown, had been living in retirement, with no wish, and with no possible means to produce an excitement against that institution. In fact, it will be seen in the course of these suggestions, that abundant causes to account for the popular excitement against the Convent had occurred immediately preceding its destruction, without any possible connection with the isolated fact that a young girl had left the institution two years and a half before, and had given to her immediate friends a narrative of the events which she witnessed there. Nevertheless, the fact that the young lady had committed such a narrative to writing, soon after she left the Convent, (although that fact was known to but very few persons, including her pastor and her immediate friends and advisers,) was magnified into very great importance, *after* the Convent was burnt. For nearly a year before that event, the manuscript of this Narrative (containing every fact precisely as it is now published) had remained undisturbed in the hands of the reverend gentleman of whose church Miss R. had become a member, after renouncing the Roman Catholic faith; and whatever intention there might have originally been of giving it publicity, all such intention had been abandoned. It would seem, therefore, to have required the utmost ingenuity of motive hunters, to have traced the burning of the Ursuline Convent in 1834 to a narrative of a six months' residence there in 1831, which a young girl had written two years before, and which had been seen in manuscript only by a very limited number of her friends.

But strange as it will be considered, on due reflection, the "little treatise" published by Martin Luther, in 1520, was not more terribly denounced by the Pope and his spiritual subjects, than has been the simple manuscript narrative of Miss R., in 1832, by the Catholics and their friends in this quarter. Even many of the apparent friends of truth, and of the religion of the New Testament, will no doubt be as much startled at the boldness of our presuming to publish this little Narrative, and will consider it "the signal for war," quite as seriously, and just as *wisely*, as did *some* of the friends of Luther, when he gave his first account of abuses and follies he had himself witnessed in the Monasteries and Convents of that day. And be it remembered too, that the statements of Luther for some time rested on his *individual* assertions against the whole hierarchy of Rome. Had Christians believed the Priests and discredited Luther, where would have been the Reformation? Shall then Christians of the present day, Christian parents who have daughters to educate, disbelieve the narrative of a residence in a modern Convent, made by a convert from that order, merely because in matters of fact which only she and the Catholic community at the institution could have witnessed, the latter attempt to discredit her testimony? Would they not do so of course, if the disclosure of the truth must open the eyes of Protestants, so as to convince them of the impropriety of intrusting the education of their daughters to a secret and superstitious community of Catholic Priests and Nuns?

It is in the hope that the truth will prevail, that we have advised the publication of this Narrative, which, just like the little treatise of Luther, has been denounced and condemned by those who know nothing of its real contents, as "heretical, scandalous, and offensive to pious ears." We doubt not that when it is published, that portion of the community and the press who have made up their minds to listen to nothing against the infallibility of Ursuline Convents to educate Protestant daughters, will not, in their denunciations, be a whit behind the damnatory bull of Pope Leo X. against Luther, for publishing his "little treatise." All persons will be forbidden to read and believe the "little" Narrative about the Convent, under pain of being held up to public odium as among the rioters, or at least abettors of the riot, which led to the destruction of the Nunnery at Mount Benedict. Even pious men and women will be so eager to show their religious *tolerance* and Christian *charity* for Catholic Nunneries, that they will labor with all their might to destroy the character of an American Protestant girl, who has escaped from Catholic superstition; in order to maintain the infallible purity of a secret community of foreign females, who have introduced among us for the imitation of the daughters of republicans, the ascetic austerities of a religious discipline destructive of all domestic and social relations.

As to those who have advised this publication, and who venture to doubt the infallibility of Convents in 1835, as Luther did the infallibility of the Pope in 1520, we anticipate, as a matter of course, from a portion of the community, all manner of denunciations and excommunications, as "obstinate heretics, fit only to be delivered unto Satan for the destruction of the flesh." Nevertheless, we very conscientiously believe that it is as much our duty to give this "little" Narrative of Convent discipline to the Christian public, as it was the duty of Luther to publish his "little treatise" three hundred years ago. We earnestly desire that the public may discriminate between the Roman Catholic religion and a Roman Catholic *school* to educate daughters of Protestants, and that they will not longer confound religious toleration with the encouragement of monastic seminaries of learning. We regard this matter as more immediately connected with the great interests of EDUCATION among us, than it is with the advancement of pure and undefiled religion. It is not a question of creeds and sects, but it is a grave question how the future ornaments to our most refined society, the future accomplished mothers of American citizens, shall be educated. We ask, in this view, is it not a startling fact, that here in the town of Charlestown, in the immediate vicinity of Boston, celebrated above all other communities for its means of giving a *Christian* and a *republican* education to its children, the aid of a foreign, ascetic, superstitious, anti-republican institution should have been called in, established solely by Roman Catholics, who have taken relivious vows of "POVERTY," and yet hold out public inducements and charge the highest prices for educating the daughters of wealthy parents of that class of Christians whom "all good Catholics" regard as heretics, who must inevitably be damned unless they are converted to the only true faith!

It is high time that a little common sense was applied to the estimate of the motives and objects of Roman Catholic monastic institutions for educating Protestant children! Many of our most influential citizens seem to be preparing the public to abandon all Protestant schools, and send their daughters to be educated in Roman Catholic Cloisters. The next step may be, that whenever a young girl, thus educated, is crossed in love, or disappointed in securing a fashionable establishment in marriage, she will turn Nun, and take the vows of the Ursuline order; and wealthy parents, who have more daughters than they can portion in the style they have been brought up, may find it convenient to persuade the least beautiful to take the veil. Such things are common among the aristocracies of Europe. Why may they not be introduced here, if public opinion is found to favor the establishment of Convents?

The highly respectable Committee appointed by the citizens of Boston, not to eulogize the Convent, but solely "to investigate the proceedings of the night of the riot, and to adopt every suitable mode of bringing the authors and abettors of the outrage to justice," say in their elaborate vindication of that institution, that "the number of pupils has varied from forty to sixty, during each of the past five years, being for the most part daughters of those among the most respectable families in the country, of various religious denominations, the number of *Catholics* never exceeding TEN at any one time. No means were taken (say the Committee) to influence or *affect* their religious opinions, nor can it be ascertained that any pupil placed under their charge for the purposes of education has been converted from any other to the Catholic faith, or induced to become a member of the Community."

The Superior of the Convent, in her testimony on the trial of the rioters, declared that the vows of her religious order are "POVERTY, chastity, and obedience; to separate themselves from the world, and to follow the instructions of the Superior." She also testified that the institution at Mount Benedict was supported by the profits of the school; that it was out of debt, and all the property paid for, besides more than a thousand dollars in cash in her private drawer, which she had not counted for a year! (an evidence of "poverty," by the way, which most people who take no vows to become paupers would rejoice to have in their possession.) She further testified that there were no funds but those arising from the pupils, and that she and her sisters in the Ursuline Community were supported out of that fund; this whole "Community," so supported, consisting of "eight Nuns and two Novices at the Convent."

Both the Superior and the Bishop testified that the property of the Nnunery which was destroyed amounted to fifty thousand dollars, exclusive of the real estate and appurtenances.

Now put these facts together, and what are we called on to believe!. Why, that a capital of at least SIXTY THOUSAND DOLLARS (which invested in stocks would have yielded a revenue of three thousand six hundred dollars annually) was set apart and put into the splendid and sumptuous establishment at Mount Benedict, for the purpose of supporting *ten* females who had taken on themselves vows of POVERTY, and also for the purpose of educating *ten* Roman Catholic children! Was there ever greater disparity between means employed and the professed ends for which those means are said to be employed?

The Nunnery, therefore, could not have been designed merely as a family residence, or as a place of worship for ten females under vows of "POVERTY," nor could so extensive an institution have been erected to educate *ten* Catholic children. Neither could the Nuns themselves be ambitious of public distinction as eminent teachers, for they had vowed "to separate themselves from the world!"

The primary object, then, must have been, not to provide

a place for the religious devotion of Roman Catholics, but to establish a seminary for the education of the daughters of Protestants. This is proved by the public advertisements of the Superior, and the agencies established in New Orleans and other cities, to procure Protestant pupils for the Charlestown Nunnery. If then it was a mere *school*, it has no claim to sanctity, and should be open to examination, like the schools of Protestants. We protest against claiming religious sanctity for a school for girls. If the Nunnery was a place for disseminating the Roman Catholic religion, then the children of Protestants should not be sent there to learn that religion. But if it was a school to educate Protestant girls, then the whole interior discipline of both pupils and teachers ought to be known.

But why should Roman Catholics establish so costly a seminary in the vicinity of Boston, to educate the daughters of Protestants? Could it have originated in the disinterested benevolence of a foreign lady, brought up in the seclusion of a Convent in Canada, who, with her five sisters similarly educated, should have taken such a deep interest in the young ladies of Boston and the United States, as to form so extensive an establishment to enable them to obtain an accomplished education?

Or could the intelligent Catholic Bishop of Boston have been so deeply impressed with the total neglect of female education in Boston and its vicinity, as to be at all this trouble and expense for the sole benefit of the daughters of heretics, without the least design, as the Boston Committee affirm, to use the slightest means to influence or *affect* their religious opinions? Neither the Bishop nor the Superior could have looked to this establishment as a source of *pecuniary* profit, because that would be to compel the Nuns to become teachers for filthy lucre, and thus violate their vow of "POVERTY!"

If, then, no mercenary views were connected with the establishment of the Nunnery, and there was no lack of good Protestant schools for Protestant females, (certainly much better than the Nunnery proved to be,) where was the motive? "It was disinterested benevolence!" say the friends of the Convent. Perhaps we could have believed it was, if the avowed object of the institution had been to convert the children of heretics to the true faith, in order to save them from eternal destruction. Look at it in this view a moment. Here were eight females having the charge of fifty amiable and interesting girls, and believing on their souls that every one of these children were miserable heretics, who must be damned to all eternity, unless they embraced the Roman Catholic faith! If the Superior and her Nuns did not honestly believe this, then their religion is a cheat or they were hypocrites. We draw no such conclusion, but doubt not they sincerely believed the infallible creed of "mother church," that these children, with all their winning attractions, must inevitably be shut out of all hopes of heaven, unless they were converted to Romanism. Could pious and benevolent ladies, day after day, and year after year, see their own children, as it were, placed in this awful peril, and not make an effort to save them from eternal destruction? What should we say of a pious clergyman, at the head of a seminary, who should have fifty boys in his school, whose parents had brought them up to deny God and ridicule the Scriptures, and yet he should boast publicly that he had "taken no means to influence or *affect* their religious opinions," and had "never exacted their attendance upon religious services?" Is not this the light in which the Boston Committee represent the Superior of the Convent and the Bishop, if they really have made no effort, for five years, to save the precious souls of fifty interesting female children, intrusted by heretics to their paternal care?

Most assuredly it is; and if what they say of the Convent in this particular be true, it takes away the last possible pretence for getting up that institution—benevolence. Had the Superior or the Bishop suffered one of the Protestant pupils to have walked in her sleep out of the window, and lost her life, when timely caution might have prevented it, with what horror the community would have heard of such an outrage. And yet the Boston Committee ask us to believe that all the Priests and Nuns at the Convent religiously believed that the fifty children they had under their daily care were walking in the sleep of spiritual death, liable every moment to fall into eternal perdition, but they would not reach forth a hand to save them! "No means were taken to influence or affect their religious opinions!" It seems to us that it would be more honorable to the establishment at Mount Benedict, to prove that it was designed to save the daughters of heretics from perdition, by making them good Catholics; and in point of fact we believe the Committee were mistaken. There are pupils from the Nunnery who declare that serious attempts were made to affect their religious opinions; and in truth could it possibly be otherwise, with ingenuous girls, living in the romantic atmosphere of a Roman Catholic Nunnery, with all the mysterious and externally imposing ceremonies of that religion constantly passing before their eyes and ears, in a portion of which they daily participated? If any one desired to possess the power of giving a color to the impressions of after life, would he ask for better means than these?

If then the object of establishing Catholic Nunneries to educate Protestant girls is neither pecuniary profit, worldly honor, or disinterested benevolence, is it uncharitable to conjecture that the real design must be to give to Catholics a controlling influence over the minds of our youth, and disseminate their tenets, by an imperceptible, winning way of not seeming to disseminate them at all? At any rate, as the education of our daughters is a matter of such vital importance to the purity of society, can we know too much of the interior discipline of an institution in which they have been placed without their parents ever being permitted to enter any part of the school or the Nunnery, except a common visiting parlor to which the pupils and their instructers are called, whenever they are seen by the public eye?

These are some of the considerations which have led to the publication of the unpretending narrative that will be found in this little book. It has been committed to the press after a long, deliberate, and, we may add, prayerful consideration of the dictates of justice, truth, and religion. The existence of such a narrative in manuscript, and various and unfounded speculations as to the nature of its contents, have been connected with the destruction of the Convent, and have given rise to many injurious and unkind misrepresentations of the motives of its author, ever since that outrage was committed. Individuals in private, and committees in public reports, have made the supposed contents of this narrative the basis of a formidable "conspiracy, extending into many of the neighboring towns," resulting in the final burning of the Convent, on the 11th of August, 1834. Others have supposed that it would disclose terrible scenes of personal profligacy and inquisitorial tortures: but both classes who have so judged have entirely misapprehended the character of the narrative, and of its author. Under these contradictory impressions, one portion of the community have been urging the immediate publication of the Narrative, while others have threatened its author, and those who should undertake its publication, with a worse excommunication and denunciation than was inflicted upon Luther for his temerity. Nevertheless, "the more thinking and judicious part of mankind," who have had an opportunity of learning the facts, have "looked upon the publication" of the whole matter "as the wisest step, even in a worldly and prudential light, which could possibly be taken to render contemptible and abortive" the attempts that have been made and are still making to silence the press, to condemn all who condemn Convents, and to injure the peace of mind and destroy the delicate reputation of the daughter of one of our native citizens, in order to justify a foreign institution established among us under the control of a hierarchy adverse to a republican form of government.

We have not believed that it became American Christians or American citizens to offer up, on the altar of a Roman Catholic Convent, the character of one of our own unoffending daughters, who, after having been drawn into the Romish Church, by the exterior romantic attractions of a Nunnery patronized by Protestants, has had the Christian fortitude to escape from the dark meshes in which her mind had been entangled, and to disclose, in the simple language of truth, all that she saw, heard, and felt, while under this delusion. From a careful examination of this subject, we are led to view it as a remarkable evidence of conscious innocence and integrity, as well as piety and firmness, that a young and delicate female, of timid and retiring habits, of extreme sensibility, and with her health seriously impaired by religious austerities and seclusion, should have been enabled to maintain so much consistency, mildness, and propriety in all she has said, written, or done in relation to her connection with the Ursuline Convent: and that too when much of the wealth and talent of this great city has been enlisted in defending and eulogizing that establishment, and in denouncing as participators in or approvers of the riot, all who called in question the sanctity of its inmates, and the propriety of Protestants sending their daughters there. We have never discovered in the feelings or language of Miss R. the slightest indication of resentment toward that Community or its Superior, nor will it be detected in any portion of her Narrative, which it seems to us no person of an unbiased mind can peruse without feeling a conviction not to be resisted, that it is the unaffected language of truth and innocence.

The circumstances under which this relation of a six months' residence in the Ursuline Convent at Charlestown, was originally prepared, and which have led to its present publication, are material in forming an estimate of the degree of credit that may confidently be attached to it. We wish it to be distinctly understood that the publication is not made at the instigation, or on the responsibility of the author. On the contrary, she has very reluctantly yielded to the force of circumstances and the dictates of duty, which, in the opinion of her friends and the friends of truth, have left no other course proper to be pursued; and has placed her manuscript at their disposal. If then there is an error of judgment in giving this work publicity, it belongs to the friends of Miss R., and to many of our most sedate and respectable citizens who have advised with them, and not to herself. The design of the publication on our part, is to vindicate her from unjust and unmanly aspersions which some friends of the Convent have indulged in toward her, and especially to advance the cause of truth. We earnestly hope and believe that this little work, if universally diffused, will do more, by its unaffected simplicity, in deterring Protestant parents from educating their daughters at Catholic Nunneries, than could the most labored and learned discourses on the dangers of Popery. And if it has this blessed effect in guarding the young women of our land against the danger of early impressions imbibed at Convents in favor of a form of religion which is to be *tolerated* but never to be *encouraged* in a free country, it will do more even than the laws can do in suppressing such outrages as the riot at Charlestown; for if Protestant parents will resolve to educate their daughters at Protestant schools, and patronize no more Nunneries, then no more Nunneries will be established in this country, and there will be none for riotous mobs to destroy.

We do not desire to interfere in any manner with the religious privileges of Roman Catholics, or with their education of their own daughters in any form they may think proper, if not inconsistent with the laws; but we earnestly hope, that Protestant parents, before they place their children under the tuition of either a College of Jesuits or a Community of Nuns and Catholic Priests, will first inquire how the proposed educators of their daughters have themselves been educated: and what the nature and effect of the absurd superstitions, the ascetic austerities, the ridiculous penances, the secret confessionals, the unchecked facilities for intrigue, which constitute the discipline of a Convent, are and *must* be upon instructers and pupils, abiding under such influences.

This little Narrative is an unaffected and plain relation of facts, upon which a correct opinion can be formed of the probable tendencies of such a system. It was commenced in 1832, and completed in the winter of 1833. Not one of those at whose suggestion it is now published had ever heard of it until after the destruction of the Convent, and we are well assured that very few persons indeed knew that it had ever been written, until after the outrage at Charlestown had been committed. It was placed in our hands, as the friends of truth, after the publicity of the personal attacks which had been made upon Miss R. with singular unkindness and injustice, through a portion of the public press, by the constant and relentless calumnies of the female superintendent of the Convent, and finally by the illiberal, and, we are compelled to add, ungenerous, Report of the Boston Investigating Committee, in which thirty-eight gentlemen of high character (every one of whom would spurn the thought of deliberately injuring an unprotected female) have been induced to give their sanction to aspersions and insinuations against a daughter of one of their own fellow-citizens, upon no evidence whatever, except that derived from and through the offended Superior of the Convent and her Community, from whom that daughter had escaped, under circumstances which, if true, render the testimony of her accusers wholly unsafe as a guide to the real character of the interior of the Nunnery.

It has been represented that the contents of Miss R.'s narrative were very monstrous, shocking, and incredible, and even the charge of aberration of mind has been resorted to, by those who would have great cause of thankfulness if they were blessed with the singleness of heart and the unaffected piety which mark the character of that young lady. Threats have even been thrown out that her character should be made to suffer if she dared to publish any thing against the Convent, and it is understood that the Boston Investigating Committee upon the destruction of the Convent were urged to retain in their Report the harsh language toward Miss R. which had been prepared by a sub-committee, in order to discredit by anticipation any statements which might thereafter be made on her authority, relative to the internal discipline of that establishment. We fully acquit the majority of that very respectable committee of any deliberate design to wound the feelings and injure the reputation of a lady. They acted under the sudden and laudable impulse of manly resentment toward the authors of a shameless outrage committed upon the residence of defenceless females; and as the ladies of the Convent were then the most prominent sufferers, and the objects of universal public sympathy, it was natural, if not excusable, that high-minded men, in their eagerness to redress their wrongs, should have become unmindful of the rights of a single individual, who was represented by the Catholics and some of their friends as the prime mover of the excitement against the Convent, by reason of the calumnies she was represented as having circulated against it.

As one of the material considerations which in our opinion has rendered the publication of this Narrative indispensable, we subjoin several extracts from the Report of the Boston Committee, which, it will be seen, directly attributes to Miss R. the principal origin of the popular excitement that led to the disgraceful catastrophe of the 11th of August.

"It appeared immediately upon commencing the investigation, that the destruction of the Convent might be attributed primarily to a widely-extended popular aversion, founded in the belief that the establishment was obnoxious to those imputations of cruelty, vice, and corruption, so generally credited of similar establishments in other countries, and was inconsistent with the principles of our national institutions, and in violation of the laws of the commonwealth; and *which aversion*, in the minds of many, *had been fomented to hatred*, by representations injurious to the moral reputation of the members of that Community, attributing to them impurity of conduct, and excessive cruelties in their treatment of each other and of the pupils; and denunciatory of the institution as hostile in its character and influence alike to the laws of God and man: and *also* by reports that one of the sisterhood, Mrs. Mary John, formerly Miss Elizabeth Harrison, after having fled from the Convent to escape its persecutions, and then been induced by the influence or threats of Bishop Fenwick to return, had been put to death, or secretly imprisoned or removed."

"The Committee have been unable to find any report in circulation injurious to the reputation of the members of the Community, which may not be traced to *one of the above sources*, or which has *any other* apparent foundation."

In another part of their Report the Committee say:—"In pursuing their inquiries into the truth of the injurious representations and reports *above* referred to, members of the Committee have had an interview with the young lady upon whose authority they were supposed to rest." And they then proceed to give the result of that interview as is derived from the young lady herself.

Again they say:—"It was doubtless under the influence of *these* feelings and impressions, that some of the conspirators were led to design the destruction of the Convent."

It will be seen therefore that this Report directly ascribes the origin of the outrage on the Nunnery to the aversion and hatred fomented by injurious representations and reports, founded upon the authority of Miss R., who had left the Convent more than two years before it was destroyed by a mob. The sub-committee who drew up the Report, in fact, attach but very little importance to the escape of Miss Harrison, (who was one of the *trustees* of the establishment,) and the exciting circumstances attending her leaving the Convent and her sudden return to it. They cast no censure on her, and impute no indiscretion to her, or to those who required her to labor so hard as a teacher as to derange her faculties. They do not inquire whether she was really deranged or not, (of which there is no direct proof, and very much against it,) and they are entirely willing to exempt her, and those who refused to explain promptly the cause of her escape, from all possible blame as the real or innocent authors of the mob; while they seriously set about affixing upon a humble Protestant girl, who had been deluded into the Catholic Church and escaped from her spiritual thraldom, all the "injurious reports" that led to the riot. Neither did the Committee inquire whether the threats of the Superior to the selectmen of Charlestown, that the Bishop could order out twenty thousand Irishmen to destroy their property; and the insults which the pupils cast upon the public authorities of the town when they visited that establishment, were not sufficient causes to account for the public excitement, without going back nearly three years, to trace the origin of a formidable conspiracy to a mere girl!

After thus preparing the public to regard with aversion a "young woman" who could have spent nearly three years in fomenting hatred against the Convent, by means of injurious reports, until she had produced an excitement that led to the commission of burglary and arson by a mob, the Report of the Committee proceeds to give a summary of the whole of her testimony a they profess to have received it from her own mouth.

And how did they arrive at their version of all that Miss R. authorized or did not authorize, relative to reports affecting the character of the Nunnery? Two members of the Committee, it seems, had *one* interview with the young lady, to whom they were entire strangers, and out of that interview they derive materials for disposing of the whole matter, in a very summary manner. It should be borne in mind that just before the Report comes to this conclusion, it deliberately asserts that the Committee were "unable to find *any* report in circulation, injurious to the members of the Convent," which was not traced either to Miss R. or to the reports which grew out of the elopement of Miss Harrison. There is then introduced a formal disclaimer for Miss R., followed by a classification of her supposed testimony, from which the Report arrives at the happy conclusion that Miss R. had in fact said nothing against the Convent amounting to any thing, and that all she did say was entirely discredited: and yet she is indirectly held up to the public odium in that Report as the author of the mob, and her testimony discredited by contrast with that of the ladies of the Convent, when by the showing of the Report itself she had said nothing really injurious to the Convent! Why then was she injured in this public manner, on the pretence that other people had circulated false reports in her name, which reports she never heard of and the Committee do not specify?

The two gentlemen of the Committee who had the interview with Miss R. say for her, that "she entirely disclaimed most of the reports passing under the sanction of her name, and particularly all affecting the moral purity of the members of the institution, or the ill treatment of the pupils under their care:" and this disclaimer is published in Italics, as if it were the precise language of Miss R. But it is not her language, nor did she ever authorize any such public disclaimer to be made for her. "Disclaimed *most* of the reports passing under the *sanction* of her name," say the Committee! If the reports had the *sanction* of her name, then she must have authorized them. But what were the *reports* passing under her name? Miss R. never heard of any reports passing under her name, except those found in her Narrative. Did the two gentlemen whom Miss R. (mistaking for friends, and not suspecting they came to get materials to injure her veracity) consented to see, though reluctantly, the *third* time they called for that purpose—did these gentlemen describe to her a single specific report as passing under her name, and ask her if it was true? If she disclaimed *most* of the reports passing under her name, what were those "*most*," and what were the remainder of the reports she did not disclaim? Could specific reports be disclaimed by her, when Miss R. was not apprized what the reports were that the Committee say were passing under the sanction of her name?

Then as to the formal disclaimer of all reports affecting the *moral purity* of the members, &c. Miss R., as the gentlemen subsequently admitted, used no such language as this. "Moral purity" is a wide phrase, and as here used it implies that Miss R. had never witnessed any thing at the Convent which was morally wrong. Had the Committee confined this disclaimer to any imputations on female virtue, they would have been correct, and would not have fallen into the error of doing great injustice to one lady, in their zeal to vindicate others. The gentlemen who called on Miss R. cannot have forgotten that she declined saying any thing on this subject, and that the language introduced into the Report is their own inference. In relation to the ill treatment of the pupils, there was no disclaimer at all. One of the gentlemen who called on Miss R. has frankly admitted this, and he would have corrected that portion of the Report, had it not been beyond his control when the error was pointed out to him. On his part a highly honorable disposition was evinced to correct the unjust advantage which had been taken of a private conversation with a lady, who had no suspicion she was undergoing a public examination, in an interview which she understood was friendly and confidential.

After these disclaimers, the Report classifies what it terms Miss R.'s "*accusations*" under the heads of "severe penance," "restraints upon members of the Community," and penances inflicted upon a Nun in her last illness, by which her life was shortened. And in order to leave no mistake in the inference that all these disclaimers and assertions are derived from Miss R. herself, as the whole sum and substance of her experience at the Convent, the Report sums up with this conclusion:—

"From HER *statement*, therefore, it is evident that there could be, except in the subject of the *last* accusation, no cause of *public* complaint, inasmuch as the other evils alleged, if existing, were confined to those who were voluntarily members of the institution, affecting neither the property nor the happiness of other individuals, nor tending in any wise to the injury of the public morals, or a violation of law."

In other words, shortening the life of a Nun by severe penances, inflicted in her "last illness," would be a cause of public complaint against a Convent; but severe penance and restraints, however destructive of health, which Nuns and Novitiates might be compelled to suffer, *before* their "*last* illness," would furnish no ground for any complaint at all, provided they survived the cruelty inflicted by superstition! Upon the same reasoning, the slow tortures of the Inquisition might have been introduced into the Monastery at Mount Benedict, and so long as they were confined to the "voluntary members," and did not result in the actual death of their victims, there would be "no cause of public complaint," because while the infernal process of cruelty was kept secret within the walls of a dungeon, it could not in any wise injure the public morals! The Bramins of the East argued in the same way against the interference of the British with the *privilege* of widows being voluntarily burned on the funeral pile of their husbands. They insisted that it "affected neither the property nor the happiness of other individuals," that it was an ancient custom, and in fact promoted the "public morals," by insuring the wife's solicitude for her husband while living, and her fidelity after his death.

Is it not also remarkable, that the Report of the Boston Committee could have come to the conclusion, that although fifty Protestant girls were placed under the entire control and instruction of a community of eight Nuns, one of whom had been obliged to labor so hard as a teacher as to drive her to madness, yet it was "no cause of public complaint," even admitting that the persons thus intrusted with giving the first impressions to young ladies were in the daily practice of superstitiously inflicting upon each other, and upon themselves, severe penances, rigorous restraints, and all the absurd cruelties imposed by monastic religious discipline?

We have no wish to say one word disrespectful to the gentlemen who signed the Report of the Boston Investigating Committee. Their motives were highly honorable. But there were some few acting in the Committee without any legitimate authority, (for the original committee had no power to increase their number,) whose zeal to vindicate the Convent and its Protestant patrons made them forget what was due to the daughter of an American citizen. This is painfully obvious in the manner in which Miss R. has been introduced into that Report, without her knowledge or consent. She was not called as a witness before the Committee, so that each might have judged of her intelligence for himself. They did not see her narrative of her residence at the Nunnery, nor did she make a single "accusation" to them against the Convent. Neither had she or her friends any notice of the written and spoken "accusations" which were made to the Committee by Mrs. Moffatt, Superior of the Convent, against Miss R.; and no opportunity was given, though it was asked for, to enable the friends of Miss R. to protect her against that portion of the Report designed to affect her character injuriously. The whole process was sending two gentlemen to converse an hour with her alone, under an assurance of friendly confidence, without apprizing her that any public use whatever was to be made of the conversation, or intimating to her that the entire truth of her relations had been or would be called in question. Though disposed to respect the motives of the gentlemen who called on Miss R., and obtained a portion of her confidence for a purpose which was certainly concealed from her at the time; they must permit us to say that they did their own high sense of honor, as well as Miss R., great injustice, when they allowed a public use to be made of a private conversation with a lady, who did not consent to see them until they called the third time, who then referred them to another person for information, and who would not have seen them at all, could she have conjectured that the object was to obtain the means of discrediting her veracity, and introducing her before the public in the unjust and unkind manner she is treated in that Report.

But the gentlemen who have mistaken the point of honor as well as justice in this transaction, have the power in their own hands, to use it as they think proper; for, unfortunately, their interview with Miss R. took place without any friend on her part being present. In fact, the strong bias of that Report to justify the Convent at the expense of all whose statements had affected it injuriously, must be apparent, when we find gentlemen of the highest character and integrity, sitting as an impartial tribunal, proceeding first to collect the asseverations of the Superior, her Nuns, and the Catholic Priests, as to the purity of their *own* conduct, and *their* version of the conduct of Miss R., who had escaped from them; then sending a committee, as private gentlemen, to call on that lady with assurances of friendly confidence and religious fellowship, and introducing into a public report the alleged results of that interview, as "*her* statement," which is used in order to show that "her statement" is not to be believed!

The only grounds on which the Committee in that Report justify their unkind treatment of Miss R., is, that "it is stated (so and so) by the ladies of the institution." This statement, which comes solely from the party accused, an impartial committee receive as conclusive evidence of the purity and propriety of all the proceedings at the Convent, and upon this evidence they discredit Miss R.

Is it not, indeed, very remarkable, that that young lady should have been the only individual singled out in the Report of the Committee, the only person whose testimony is formally stated in order to be discredited, especially when it is recollected that she was the only person who was acquainted with the interior discipline of the Convent, and whose evidence could be used to disclose any thing wrong, if any thing wrong existed there? The Committee had no such design, but how natural was it for the friends of the Superior, imbibing her strong dislike to a seceder from the Convent, to infuse into the Report an ingredient of malice which to the whole Committee bore the semblance of truth. The Attorney-General, in his eloquent denunciation of the rioters, said that the age of chivalry was gone here, for no one stepped forward to rescue the property of the Convent from a mob. Was there any less want of chivalry when thirty-eight gentlemen brought all their influence to bear against a young lady, and condemned her *unheard?*

It was on the appearance of this Report, reflecting upon the character of a young lady, (who had apparently committed no error, except suffering her romantic credulity to lead her to renounce the religion in which she had been brought up, for the supposed sanctity and seclusion of a Nunnery,) that a number of her friends and the friends of truth felt that something was due to a defenceless daughter of one of our own citizens, and that she ought not to be exposed to censure for disclosing any facts connected with the Convent, if they were such as ought to put Protestant parents on their guard against educating their daughters at Catholic Cloisters.

They began to doubt whether something was not wrong, when they found it a part of the plan of those most zealous in eulogizing the Convent, to destroy the reputation of a female who had returned to the Protestant faith, and whose only faults were that her religion had been affected by Catholic influence, that it led her to become a novitiate in the Convent, that she had left it as soon as she became sensible of the tendency of such a system of religious discipline as was practised there, and had not shrunk from telling the plain truth to her friends and her religious teacher in explanation of her own conduct during her connection with the Nunnery. It was understood that great efforts had been made by a portion of the Investigating

Committee, aided by the amiable and pious clergyman before alluded to, to exclude from the Report all direct allusion to Miss R.; and but for the earnestness with which the sacrifice of that young lady was urged by a few, this desirable object would have been accomplished, and the publication of Miss R.'s narrative been rendered unnecessary for her vindication. The same facts and arguments to rebut the supposed allegations against the Convent might have been introduced into the Report, without any personal reference to Miss R. But it seems to have been the design of a portion of that Report, (in which, however, we are satisfied but a small number of the Committee participated,) to attribute all the stories injurious to the Convent to Miss R., to represent her as the author of monstrous, undefined calumnies, and then make use of a conversation held with her, in the absence of all her friends, to discredit her testimony generally, and in all matters resting upon her statement on one side, and the contradiction of the female superintendent of the Convent on the other, to give a decided preponderance in public opinion to the latter.

Nevertheless, though the injustice of this proceeding was apparent to those best acquainted with the real facts in the case, it was equally apparent that while the excitement consequent on the infamous outrage upon the property of the owners and occupants of the Convent was at its height, it would be in vain to appeal to the public for a candid estimate of the real merits of the case at issue. It was also considered, that it might be regarded as an attempt to influence the public in relation to the important trials then pending, should such an appeal be made through the public press. The injustice, therefore, was submitted to in silence, until the public mind should be quieted, and a legal examination, under oath, take place of the ex parte and exaggerated investigation which had been held before the Boston Committee, who had embodied the vague stories of voluntary witnesses, related not under oath, but in secret, under an assurance that the names of the witnesses were to be concealed, so that whether they testified truly or falsely they were certain of being shielded from all responsibility. In short, it was the determination of the friends of Miss R., in conformity with her wishes, not to give publicity to her narrative, unless it became indispensable to the cause of truth, nor then, until such disposition had been made of the pending prosecutions of the rioters, as to render such a course free from all just imputation of an attempt to interfere with the public justice.

Scarcely, however, had those trials before the Supreme Court sitting at Cambridge terminated, when a still more unjust attempt was made to injure the character of Miss R., and hold her up to public indignation as the prime mover of the conspiracy which led to the destruction of the Ursuline Convent. This wholly unprovoked attack came from a person of high standing in the community, holding the office of judge of probate of the county of Middlesex, who had been for six years a patron of the Convent, and one of the most zealous defenders of the faith that Catholic Nunneries were the best schools for the education of the daughters of republican Protestants. The peculiar relation in which that individual stood to the Convent will best appear by quoting the language of the respectable counsel for the defendant in the trial of John R. Buzzell.

Mr. Mann, one of the counsel, said to the jury—"I do not think Judge Fay is sensible his feelings are excited, but it seems to me that he comes here highly excited. Is it not strange that he can recollect the voice [of the prisoner] and not a word that he said? He thinks that the prisoner is guilty, and that blood should be shed, and I submit, that every thing *he* sees and hears operates to the prejudice of the prisoner."

Mr. Farley said—"I would next call your attention to Judge Fay's testimony; and in the outset I tell you, without any unfavorable feeling toward Judge Fay, whom I highly esteem, that he does not know himself, he does not know his own feelings, or he would not have told you that he could have tried a person for this crime immediately after, with impartiality. Both Mr. Thaxter and Judge Fay are insensibly under the influence of feeling in this matter, arising from their having friends at the Convent, and being themselves the supporters and patrons of the institution, and having entire confidence in its excellency and purity. Believing so, and having placed their children there, it was natural they should wish to prove the institution a good one. These circumstances justify the belief, that Judge Fay, as high as his character stands, cannot possibly be an impartial witness in this cause."

It was under these impressions, and an apparent extreme irritation at the acquittal of Buzzell, that Judge Fay published a communication in the Boston Courier of January 5, 1835, in which he recklessly charged the editor of that paper, as the editor himself says, "with a direct agency in producing the destruction of the Convent."

It will also be seen, by the following extract, that in the beginning of his letter he attributes the mob to a paragraph in the newspapers, while in the close he represents the destruction of the Convent as the object and result of the "pious labors" of Miss R. for the last two or three years.

Extract from Judge Fay's Letter.

"I verily believe there would have been no mob on Monday night, but for the paragraph first published in the Mercantile Journal of Saturday, and copied into the Courier of Monday, headed "*mysterious.*" And here let me say, that the editors of those papers have never, as I believe, made any apology for the publication of that paragraph, which may have been the immediate cause of the outrages of that night. The editor of the Journal has even undertaken to justify it, and to complain of being injured by the very gentle rebuke for it, contained in the Report of the Boston Investigating Committee. I would now only ask, whether any respectable editor in Boston would dare to publish such a paragraph implicating the character or conduct of the humblest citizen, upon no better authority than mere street rumor?"

Immediately after uttering this indignant rebuke against editors for implicating the character and conduct of even the *humblest* citizen, upon no better authority than *street rumor*, the judge illustrates the influence of his own moral maxim upon himself, by proceeding forthwith to indite a gross and unprovoked libel upon a respectable young lady, without having even so much as the authority of "street rumor" for the calumnies he has published.

Conclusion of Judge Fay's Letter to the Editor of the Courier of Jan. 5, 1835.

"The causes which led to the destruction of the Convent—the circumstances attending the transaction—the difficulty of bringing the actors to justice, are fit subjects for the investigation of the philosophic historian. The extraordinary fact, that while John R. Buzzell, the New Hampshire brickmaker, recently accused, tried, and acquitted, as one of the incendiaries, had his pockets filled with money, and received such other marks of popular sympathy and acknowledgment for his services and sufferings in the cause of true religion, as to demand of him a public card of thanks, no minister or member of a Protestant society in the country, as far as I have heard, has ever proposed a contribution for the unfortunate Ursulines who lost their all by this flagrant violation of their rights; this is matter for 'our special wonder.' The time will come, I trust, when all these matters will be rightly understood. As to the state of popular feeling which produced this catastrophe, if that be a mystery, a careful review of some of the religious journals of the day may in part explain it. On that point, I will take the liberty to refer you to a certain Miss Rebecca Theresa Reed, alias Rebecca Mary Agnes Theresa Reed, (as Goldsmith says, I love to give the whole name,) a Catholic Protestant, as she termed herself in court the other day, who has been about Boston and the vicinity for the last two or three years, announcing herself as 'the humble instrument in the hands of Providence to destroy the institution at Mount Benedict.' As the great object of her pious labors has been accomplished, I doubt not she will be *proud* to inform you how she did it. It is possible that a book which it is rumored she is about to publish relative to the Nunnery, may afford the desired information; but as there is reason to apprehend that the manuscript, which has been extensively read, may undergo considerable pruning and purgation to suit the views of the publisher, it is quite doubtful if you will be able to get the whole truth, or indeed any unvarnished truth, by reading it. I should therefore advise to apply directly to herself. If she be as obliging and communicative since, as she was before the achievement of the great work, I doubt not that you may be very much enlightened in all the remaining unexplained mysteries connected with a transaction, which has left an indelible stain on the character of this part of the country; exciting the grief of our friends and the pity of our enemies.

I have travelled a step or two beyond the limited object

of this communication, but I trust my motive, which is truth, and the correction of error, will be thought a sufficient justification.

Your obedient servant,

SAMUEL P. P. FAY.

Cambridge, Jan. 2, 1835.

Up to this period, Miss R. had never published a line relating to the Convent, nor authorized any publication that had been made. Her situation unavoidably subjected her to many painful inquiries, (among others to those of the lady of Judge Fay himself,) but it is believed that she uniformly conducted with a discretion and prudence in relation to any statement she has made, which it would be difficult for any young lady in her situation to excel. All the excitement attendant upon her escape from the Convent, if there ever were any, had subsided long before Miss Harrison eloped from that place, and returned under circumstances furnishing abundant materials for popular excitement.

The escape of Miss R., in 1832, was never mentioned in a single newspaper, nor made known to any but her friends, and no public allusion was ever made to it, until after the burning of the Convent. On the other hand, the elopement of Miss Harrison, in 1834, was immediately made the subject of newspaper mystery and speculation; and yet Miss R. is censured as the enemy of the Convent, and Miss Harrison applauded as its friend! Miss R. certainly has much the highest claim to the praise of discretion. Her elopement never got into the newspapers, as greedy as news catchers would have been to have seized it. But other real or pretended elopements from the Convent, previous to that of Miss R., were made matter of comment in the newspapers, so as to call for a public denial on the part of the friends of the institution, as will be seen by the following, from the organ of the Catholics in Boston.

[From the Jesuit of July 23, 1831.]

"A lying report has been for some time going the rounds of the Calvinistic presses, relative to the elopement of a [illegible] girl from the Mount Benedict Institution at Charlestown. False! false!! false!!! Messrs. Parsons, you know it to be so."

The inference, therefore, is obvious, that Miss R. avoided

any publicity that would lead to an excitement against the Convent. For nearly three years before the destruction of the Convent, she had been living in the bosom of her own family, an exemplary member of the Episcopal Church, industriously applying herself, as far as her shattered health would admit, to acquiring and giving instruction to young ladies in music and ornamental work. To suppose for a moment that a mere girl, not twenty years of age, and so situated, could possess the power, or the means, or the disposition to do what the Boston Committee and Judge Fay so unjustly attribute to her agency, viz. "fomenting to hatred the popular aversion" against the Convent, "by representations injurious to the moral reputation of the members of that Community," and forming a conspiracy "to destroy the institution at Mount Benedict," "as the great object of her pious labors," requires a credulity not surpassed by that which enables a devout Catholic actually to believe in the identical transubstantiation of a wafer into the flesh of the Savior! It would disparage the common sense of Judge Fay, much more of the Boston Committee, to suppose they believe any such thing. And yet, in grave documents emanating from both these sources, we find a young girl, moving in the humble walks of life, whose character is without reproach, charged with designing for three years, and carrying forward to its completion, in the midst of her simple avocation as the affectionate teacher of female children in music, a monstrous conspiracy to get up a mob to destroy the Ursuline Convent by violence! If these intelligent gentlemen have really brought their minds to compass such an absurdity as this, they might be brought to invert one of the miracles of sacred writ, and believe that Jonah swallowed the whale, and not that the whale swallowed Jonah!

It was not until this publication of Judge Fay appeared, that Miss R. fully consented that her friends should publish her narrative, as the only means of placing before the public all she had said and written in relation to the Convent, from which it might be seen how injuriously she had been misrepresented. The Report of the Boston Committee, though extremely unkind in other respects, was so far decorous as to omit using her name. Judge Fay was destitute of this ordinary courtesy due to every reputable female who does not bring herself voluntarily before the public. To repel his harsh imputations at once, seemed indispensable, and they were replied to by the following communication in the Boston Courier of January 7, 1835, which will explain many things connected with the narrative.

REPLY TO JUDGE FAY.

Boston, January 5, 1835.

TO THE EDITOR OF THE COURIER:

SIR,—I have been much surprised by seeing, in a letter signed "Samuel P. P. Fay," published in your paper of this morning, a violent attack upon myself, making statements *wholly false*, and adding inferences, which, I take it upon myself to say, *no honest* and *unprejudiced man* would be guilty of, even in his own thoughts, and much less in a letter sent to a public journal for publication. Much as I am averse to allowing my name to come before the public, in any manner, I cannot, in justice to myself, remain silent when such a gross calumny has been put forth; and done, too, by one whose *office* gives him a claim to respect in this community. In answering the calumnies contained in the communication of Judge Fay, it will be necessary to enter a little into particulars. In the first place, the judge "takes the liberty" to refer to me, as one who is able to give some information upon the causes of the "popular feeling" which produced the destruction of the Convent. In answer to this reference, I can only say, that it is impossible for me to account for the popular feeling *in any other manner* than that in which the learned judge himself accounted for it, when on the stand and under oath, viz. to the circumstances attending the escape of Mrs. Mary John. He then stated (under oath) that he knew of *no other cause* for the excitement which had caused the catastrophe. I can say with equal sincerity, that *I also* know of no other cause; and that to have it ascribed to me, as having in the *least degree* contributed to the excitement, is as base a calumny as was ever fabricated.

My conversation with regard to that institution, since I left it, has been confined to very few persons. No conversation of importance, with regard to it, had ever been held by me (up to the time of its destruction) with but two persons. One of them is the reverend gentleman of whose church I am now a member, and the other is a resident in the country. I have sometimes been pressed with questions concerning it, but have always avoided them as much as possible; and though I have answered some questions, I have not (up to the time above mentioned) given any information with regard to the institution, (to any other than the gentlemen before named,) further than general statements; such as, that I did not approve of the institution, and should not advise any of the young ladies among my friends to go there; that I disapproved of the discipline of the institution, thinking much of it to be too severe.

So careful have I been *not to be in any measure* the cause of an excitement against that institution, that I did not permit even my own sisters to read the manuscript which I had written concerning it. And now, that it should be publicly said of me, by one who holds a seat upon the judge's bench, that I have been the cause of the "popular feeling" of which he speaks, is an invasion of defenceless female innocence, if possible, more barbarous than that invasion of private rights, which has called forth so much public discussion.

The learned judge says I "termed" myself, when in court, a "Catholic Protestant"—for the purpose, no doubt, of holding me up to ridicule. In answer to this small wit, it is only necessary to say, that such an expression is a contradiction in terms which I did not make use of. I stated, that I was a Catholic Episcopalian; and I say so still.

But the most important misrepresentation which the judge has done me the honor to make, is in a paragraph to which he puts quotation marks, as if the words were actually mine. In answer to this, in the first place I would state, that all which is exceptionable in the paragraph *is false.* With regard to the origin from which this paragraph has been made, it will be necessary to mention a few details. About a year ago, Mrs Fay was (apparently) quite desirous to have some conversation with me upon that institution: to this end, she sent me two notes requesting me to call on her for that purpose. I had (as above stated) always endeavored to avoid particular conversation upon the subject; but in this instance, knowing that Mrs. Fay had a daughter in the institution, I thought it my duty to give her all the information I could with propriety. I therefore answered her first note, informing her that if she would call on me, I would give her all the information in my power. To this she sent another note, again requesting me to call on her: of which last I took no notice, being thankful that she wanted the information so little, as to give me an excuse for not giving it. A short time after, however, I went there to obtain a piano-forte, which I had been informed could be had upon application: I was in hopes that I should not see Mrs. Fay, but was disappointed. She immediately commenced asking me a variety of questions about the Convent, and I could not avoid having some conversation with her upon the subject. I answered her questions in general terms, as I had previously answered similar questions to other persons, without entering into any particulars, and ending the conversation as soon as politeness would permit. Previous to leaving, however, some general remarks were made on both sides; and upon her part some remarks directed to me, of a more kindly nature than any which she had previously made. In this connection I said, that "I hoped to be a humble instrument in the hands of Providence of *showing my friends the truth.*" This is what *was* said, and nothing *different* was said. The remark applied to me by Judge Fay I *never made,* nor any thing nearer to it than the one above quoted. Thus it will be seen, that yourself is not the only one to whom the learned judge has done *great injustice*.

With regard to the manuscript which the judge speaks of, it is true that I have written one; but that it has been "extensively read," is *not* true. Whether it will be published or not, it is unnecessary to answer. If however it should be published, there will be no "pruning or purgation," as is feared by the learned judge, but it will, on the contrary, be more full and explicit than was originally intended; for when written, it was not intended for publication.

I am, very respectfully, your obedient servant,

R. THERESA REED.

We take it for granted that no person, of ordinary good breeding, can justify the rude and unprovoked attack which a dignified judge, who is *legally* the *guardian* of the orphan, has made upon an orphan girl, in this communication to the editor of the Courier. What manly feeling, or what sense of justice, could have prompted this sneer? —"a certain Miss Rebecca Theresa Reed, *alias* Rebecca Mary Agnes Theresa Reed; as Goldsmith says, I love to give the whole name." Why did not the judge, while in this witty humor, exercise his ridicule upon the Lady Superior, who styled herself, when in court, by the *whole* name of "Mrs. President, Ma Mere, Mary Ann, Ursula, Lady Superior, Edmond, St. George, Moffatt?" The judge himself is not *deficient* in names!

Not content with this, the judge totally misrepresents a fact, in saying that Miss R. termed herself, in court, "a "Catholic Protestant." She did not. Chief Justice Shaw asked her, as he did all the female witnesses, "Are you a Catholic? Her answer was, I am a Catholic Episcopalian. *Chief Justice.* Do you believe in the Catholic Church? *Ans.* 'I believe in the Holy Catholic Church,' but not in the Roman Catholic Church. *Chief Justice.* Do you acknowledge the supremacy of the Pope? *Ans.* No, Sir, by no means; I am a member of the Protestant Episcopal Church."—It would seem difficult to find materials for ridicule in answers so proper and becoming as these.

But the most remarkable part of the judge's letter, is the proof he gravely gives of Miss R.'s design to burn down the Convent, by the assertion that some two years before the riot, she declared that "she hoped to be a humble instrument, in the hands of Providence, to *destroy* the institution at Mount Benedict:" and this, infers the judge, is conclusive evidence that a girl of nineteen was then getting up a conspiracy to burn down the Convent!

What a terrible incendiary Martin Luther must have been, on this principle, for when threatened with persecution from Rome, he wrote to Spalatinus—"Let them condemn me and burn my books, and if in return I do not publicly condemn and *burn* the whole mass of pontifical law, it will be *because I cannot find fire*. The Lord will, I doubt not, finish his own work, either through me as his *instrument* or through another."

In truth, the Lord did make Luther the instrument of *destroying five hundred and seventy-six* monastic establishments in Eugland alone, the annual revenues of which, to the Monks and Nuns with their vows of "*poverty*," were £132,000, more than half a million of dollars, besides plate and jewels to the value of £100,000 more! In fact, as the history of those times says, "one of the first effects of the Reformation was the destruction of the religious houses."

Was that any reason that Luther should have held his peace? The Boston Committee think so in their Report, for they say, "there can be no doubt that a conspiracy was formed, extending into many of the neighboring towns, but the Committee are of opinion that it embraced very few of respectable character in society, though *some such* may be accounted *guilty of an offence no less heinous, morally considered*, in having *excited the feelings* which led to the design."

Here in one sentence we have all the authors of statements injurious to the Nunnery, whether true or false, including Dr. Beecher for preaching against Popery, shook up together in the same bag with the rioters who set fire to the Convent! Verily Martin Luther was a rioter instead of a reformer, for he "excited the feelings" that led to very many bloody wars and persecutions, in which all Europe was involved for years.

Protestant American citizens, who regard it as a *heinous moral offence* to tell the truth and expose the danger and folly of educating the daughters of free republicans at Catholic Convents, must assuredly approve of the eulogium the infidel historian Hume pronounces on Pope Leo the Tenth, "whose sound judgment, moderation, and temper were well qualified to retard the progress of the Reformation."

Miss R. therefore, even had she used the precise language Judge Fay ascribes to her, might have quoted an illustrious example. Luther had seen the abuses of the Romish Church, as she had seen those of the Convent at Charlestown, and when his enemies proposed to stipulate for his silence, and even his friends feared he was going too far, he exclaimed, "I will not be guilty of an impious silence, and of the neglect of divine truth, and of so many thousand precious souls." And yet Luther's single assertion stood for some time against the testimony of the whole hierarchy of Rome, and had Christians taken their denials where would have been the Reformation? So if the Protestants of the present day admit the denials of the members of Catholic Convents as conclusive against the statements of all seceders from such institutions, who alone can carry into the world a knowledge of its secret discipline, will it not amount to an entire immunity to such establishments for any abuses or follies they may practise?

But it is not true that Miss R. took any pains to disseminate her opinions of the Nunnery. On the contrary, she uniformly refrained from doing so, unless under circumstances where she felt called upon by a sense of duty and the inquiries of those interested in knowing the truth. One of the few conversations she held on this subject, after she left the Convent, was the one which Judge Fay has brought before the public, and misrepresented, with marked disregard to delicacy, because the conversation he uses to establish his charge of conspiracy against Miss R. was held with *his own wife*, at her urgent solicitation. This we will prove. In 1833, Miss R. was a pupil in the Cambridgeport Academy, nearly opposite the residence of Judge Fay. Mrs. Fay called on her there, and requested an interview relative to the Convent, in which she had daughters. Miss R. declined calling. The earnestness with which the interview was pressed, will appear from the following notes, which the judge has obliged the friends of Miss R. to publish.

"Mrs. Fay will be at home this morning, and would be happy to have a few moments' conversation with Miss Reed after school this morning, if it would be agreeable to Miss Reed, in relation to the Convent. Mrs. Fay only wishes to know if certain reports which she has heard are true.

"*Friday morning.*"

[Miss R. replied in a note, declining to call at the residence of Mrs. F., but expressing a willingness to have that lady call on her. The answer to this note was as follows.]

"Mrs. Fay will not be able to call and see Miss Reed this afternoon, as she is going to Boston. She is much obliged to Miss Reed for her polite note, and will be happy to have Miss Reed call any day next week, either before or after school.

"*Saturday morning.*"

A conversation, drawn from an artless young lady, by such earnest and kind solicitations as these, certainly ought not to have been treasured up nearly two years, and then made public, in a distorted form, in order to charge upon her a conspiracy to incite a mob to commit arson and burglary.

We know it has been thrown out, by way of threat, that should Miss R. suffer her narrative to be published, her veracity would be destroyed by means of spies in the guise of friends, who had watched her ever since she escaped from the Convent, and taken down her conversations in writing, in order to detect her in some contradictions. That such a cold-blooded, jesuitical system of espionage can have been introduced into this enlightened community, and practised for the ruin of a young lady, we shall believe when we see these pretended records of Miss R.'s conversation published, and not before. We certainly acquit so respectable a lady as Mrs. F. of any design to entrap Miss R. by kind solicitations into a conversation that was to be used, at some future period, to her injury.

But there is one fact which we cannot withhold in this connection, as it will account for the spirit of extreme hostility with which Miss R. has been pursued, ever since her escape from the Convent, and her renunciation of the Roman Catholic faith. We quote from the "Jesuit," published in Boston, the organ of Romanism in New England, from which it will be seen that whenever a Catholic changes his religion, the dogma of the church enjoins that he is never afterward to be trusted or believed in any thing; and is to be driven, by persecutions, to intemperance, madness, or suicide. That these are the terrors held out to apostates from Popery, cannot be mistaken from the following language.

[From the Boston Jesuit of 1831.]

"Whenever a Catholic changes his religion, his motives and conduct are to be *invariably suspected*, and his *honesty* to be *never trusted*. Never did such *apostates* become thereby more moral or religious. Faith being the free gift of God to man, may be lost by an individual not keeping it active by the performance of the moral and religious, duties which an incarnate God and his Church inculcate and enforce.

But conscience, with her thousand tongues, will cry out in the midst of festive gayety, in darkness or solitude, against such *deep and damning perfidy*, and the unfortunate *victim*, in all the abasement of guilt, to palliate his *mental torture*, will *have recourse to the stupefying bowl*, or *terminate his career by suicide*."

Need we marvel that "mother Church" is infallible in the eyes of her votaries, when such are the arguments used against a Catholic turning Protestant? Need we wonder if even deranged fugitives from Convents should be suddenly restored to their senses, and voluntarily return to their mental prison, as the only means to escape such a terrible anathema? How conveniently, in case of the *sudden* death of an "apostate" this doctrine of a guilty conscience impelling to suicide would "cover it all over like a cloak." We bring no accusation; we merely trace avowed doctrines to their legitimate consequences; and we ask, if the above article really embodies the true spirit with which the Nuns of the Convent, the Bishop and Priests, and the Catholics generally, view the secession of Miss R. from their order, ought she not to be an object of the lively sympathy, and the zealous protection of Protestant Christians, instead of being pursued and persecuted by *them* also, as the unconscious instruments of the vengeance of the former?

One word as to the intimation that the Narrative of Miss R., as now published, has undergone "pruning and purgation to suit the publisher" It has neither been pruned nor expurgated, to suit the views of any body. It contains every fact which it contained when committed to writing by Miss R. between two and three years ago. The form in which it is now published is a revision of the original draft by Miss R., under the advice of judicious friends, but the language, the thoughts, the facts and the inferences are wholly her's, with a few unimportant corrections. We repeat, that not a fact contained in the original Narrative has been suppressed, and these are all the facts which Miss R. has at any time authorized to "pass under the sanction of her name." If she knows facts more injurious to the character of the Convent, they have not been disclosed; and a discreet public can judge from this Narrative with how much justice the Boston Committee, in their Report, have ascribed to Miss R. the origin of the excitement that led to the riot of the 11th of August.

We cannot so well describe the circumstances under which the Narrative was at first prepared, as they are related in the following communication on that subject, addressed to us by Miss R. last October.

TO MY RESPECTED FRIENDS:

Soon after I left the Ursuline Community on Mount Benedict, Charlestown, I felt it my duty and privilege to resume the connection which, before I became a convert to Romanism, I held with the Protestant Episcopal Church, in Cambridge. I accordingly applied to the Rev. Mr. C., the pastor of Christ Church, Boston, with whom I had consulted previously to my joining the Catholics. I related to him, as my pastor and spiritual adviser, the circumstances which led to the temporary renunciation of the faith in which I was brought up by my pious mother.

Before the death of my mother, she took care to have myself and two sisters baptized, at the Episcopal Church in Cambridge, by the Rev. Mr. Doane, then of Trinity Church, Boston, now an Episcopal Bishop of New Jersey.

It was the daily prayer of my beloved mother that her children might be brought up in the ways of religion and truth Accordingly she gave my two younger sisters and myself to the Episcopal Church in baptism. Previous to her death she summoned us to her bed, in presence of my father and one of our sponsors, and reminded us of the solemn obligation we had taken on ourselves in the ordinance of baptism, and said that she knew of no truer religion than that of the Church of England; that if there was a holier people, we had only to seek, and we should find them. And here I should do well to call to mind other advice and requests which she made: although her body sleeps in the dust, the remembrance of her dying words is still fresh in my mind.

When I threw off the strong delusion under which I had been induced to embrace Romanism or the Catholic religion, and my mind was left at liberty to reflect on the dying words of my departed mother, I sought consolation in the Episcopal Church. In doing this, and in applying to the Rev. Mr. C. for readmission to the church, I felt it my duty, in returning as a lost sheep to the fold, to open my whole heart, and disclose all the circumstances that led to my wandering from the truth and embracing the Roman Catholic faith—my introduction to the Ursuline Community—a narrative of my residence there—the circumstances which caused me to doubt the purity of their faith and practice—my consequent elopement from the Convent, and my renunciation of Romanism. And my present pastor can bear me witness that I have never expressed any desire to injure the Convent or bring unjust reproach on the Catholic religion, but to do my duty as I conscientiously believed I ought to do, in telling the truth, on my application for readmission to the Episcopal Church; and leave the event to the wise Disposer of all things.

At the time I related the facts contained in this Narrative to the Rev. Mr. C , he advised me as soon as I was able to put in writing all that I had learned and experienced of Roman Catholicism while among them, and while in the Convent. At first I was able to make only memoranda, but I have at last endeavored, in my own simple language, to place them together in something like the form of a narrative, for your perusal.

The above are the circumstances under which this short account has been drawn up; and I have now explained to you the motives for this narrative of the most interesting and distressing period of my life.

R. THERESA REED.

Among the many unkind things said of Miss R., an attempt has been made to impute ingratitude to her, because she was received at the Convent as a charity scholar. Mrs. Moffatt, the Superior, in her testimony, said, "Miss R. was received from motives of charity;" and the Report of the Boston Committee, taking the alleged fact solely from the Superior, says, "her means of knowledge were derived from her having become a voluntary inmate of the house, for the purpose of receiving a *gratuitous* education."

Had disinterested benevolence been the motive which led to the admission of Miss R. to the Convent, those who could exercise such benevolence would not have publicly reproached her with ingratitude on that score. But the Superior proved, while under oath, that the object was not charity, but the pecuniary interest of the school. We quote the following from the cross examination of the Superior, in answer to questions put by Mr. Farley.

"Miss Reed came as a charity scholar. She was employed in attending to her education. *Question.* What was the *design* of educating her? *Answer. To prepare her to instruct in the school. Mr. Farley.* Then after she was taught sufficiently to instruct in the school, would she not have been an *acquisition* to the Community? *Answer. Certainly.*"

This is the same kind of *charity* which a master bestows upon his apprentice the first six months. Miss R., when she applied for admission to the Convent, was found to possess a fine talent for music, which she has since developed. As an instructer in music, therefore, had she remained at the Convent after the six months, her services would have been highly important. The receipts from sixty scholars were not less than ten thousand dollars per annum, and there were but eight teachers, so that Miss R.'s proportion of labor, when qualified to instruct in music, would have been twelve hundred per annum. "Charity" like this was certainly casting a single loaf of bread upon the waters, with a certainty of receiving a whole cargo in return.

Nor was this all. Miss R. was well skilled in ornamental needle-work, as the ornaments of the altar and the robe of the Bishop can bear witness, and her industry in that department was a lull equivalent for all the "charity" she received at the Convent. We will prove this out of the mouths of the Catholics themselves, by quoting the following article referring to Miss R. just before she entered the Convent.

[From the Boston Jesuit of August 6, 1831.]

"We have frequently heard and noticed the anti-christian prejudice which a conversion from sectarianism to the Holy Catholic Church, produces in the minds of the unconverted friends and relatives of the new convert.

"A young lady (meaning Miss R.) who lived not a great distance from Boston became a convert a few months ago. This so exasperated her father, that she was obliged to leave the house. She found a shelter in the house of a worthy Catholic family. *She is very capable of obtaining a livelihood, by her knowledge of the various branches of needle-work.* Passing over a certain bridge, not very far from this city, she was met by a brother, who unnaturally exclaimed that *very little would induce him to throw her into the water.* He fortunately did not violate the majesty of the law. Happy privilege of the private judgment principle! edifying demonstration of its practical results! Read the Bible and judge for yourself, says the minister. When one does so, and thereby becomes a Catholic, he is forthwith denounced, yes, and but too often persecuted. Strange logic this! happy coincidence of principle and practice!"

We have introduced this extract merely to show that before Miss R. was received into the Convent, it was well understood by her Catholic friends, that she was very capable of obtaining a livelihood, by the precise kind of skill which was particularly wanted in the decorations of the Convent. But as this extract from the Jesuit contains many false statements never derived from Miss R. or her friends, but invented by the Priest who wrote it, we subjoin the following declaration made by the brother of Miss R., which is also fully assented to by her father.

The subscriber is the only brother of R. Theresa Reed, who was in the Convent at Charlestown for some time. He and all the family were always opposed to Theresa's going to the Convent, and did all they could to persuade her not to go there, but never used any other means than advice. Theresa was living at home with my father, and was under no necessity to seek admission to the Convent as a charity to her. We always believed she was overpersuaded by others to go there Her father always opposed her going there He showed me, at the time, a letter from the Superior of the Convent to him, which said, "With your approbation I shall receive your daughter, and give her two or three quarters' instruction and fit her for a teacher" My father did not consent, but told me he had sent word by Mrs. Locke, who did washing at the Convent, to tell the Superior not to receive his daughter, and that she had friends to provide for her.

A short time before my sister went into the Convent, I met her on Charlestown bridge, the only time I ever remember meeting her there. I tried to persuade her from going into the Convent, which she seemed very anxious to do, and wished me to go with her to see the Superior. I declined doing so, and said I should rather follow her to her grave than have her go there. In that and no other conversation I never used any threat toward her, which it would have been impossible for me to do at any time; and the story which afterwards appeared in the Jesuit, that I had threatened to throw her off the bridge, or used any threat, is a falsehood from beginning to end.

WM. C. REED, Jr.

Many persons who will read this Narrative, and have read the Boston Report, may suppose that they are called upon to decide between the veracity of the influential citizens who signed that report, and so humble an individual as Miss R. It is not so. These gentlemen do not assert a single fact or belief, in their own knowledge, which affects the correctness of Miss R.'s statement. Wherever there is any contradiction in matter of fact, it rests between Miss R. and the inmates of the Convent, relating to facts of a secret nature, which none but the Nuns, the Novitiates, and the Priests could know. The Superior, when under oath, admitted that Miss R. "would know every thing which took place during the time she was with us, excepting what occurred in the school room."

It is therefore simply a question of personal veracity, and of internal and external evidence of truth. Such being the case, and Miss R. having been presented in an unfavorable and unjust light, in the Report of the Boston Committee, it has seemed to her friends that it was due to her and due to truth, that the estimation in which she is held by those who know her best, should be made public at this time, as ample proof that she has friends to protect her from injustice.

The subjoined certificates were given shortly after the publication of the Report of the Boston Committee, and though many more, respectable names, might be obtained, the number and character of those given must satisfy every candid mind, that few young ladies of twenty, in any circle, could produce better evidence of their being entitled to confidence and esteem.

I hereby certify that Miss Rebecca T. Reed has been, for more than two years last past, a communicant at Christ Church; that I have always regarded her as a devout person and exemplary in her Christian walk and conversation; that I repose great confidence in her sincerity and intention to relate, on all occasions, what she believes to be the truth.

WILLIAM CROSWELL,
Rector of Christ Church, Boston.

October 20th, 1834.

Cambridgeport, *October 3d*, 1834.

This certifies that Miss R. Theresa Reed attended the Cambridgeport Academy several months within the last year. It gives me pleasure to add, that so far as my knowledge extended, her conduct during this time was uniformly good.

SAMUEL ADAMS,
Principal of Cambridgeport Academy

We the subscribers, having been acquainted with Miss Rebecca Theresa Reed, previous to her becoming a member of the Ursuline Community at Mount Benedict, Charlestown, and since leaving that institution, feel it due to the cause of truth and justice to say, that we consider her a person entitled to our confidence, sustaining as she does a character distinguished for love of truth, for unexceptionable morals, and for meek and modest deportment. And we feel it our duty to give, and cheerfully do give, this our testimonial, to be used by her and her friends as they shall deem most expedient.

September 26, 1834.

Boston.—James Day, Ebenezer F. Gay.

Lexington.—Jonathan Munroe, Rhoda Munroe, Susan E. Munroe, John Viles, Sally D. Viles, Sarah H. Viles, William L. Smith, Solomon Harrington, Betsey Harrington.

Woburn.—Luke Wyman, Ruth Wyman, Ruthy B. Wyman, Lucy Wyman, Seth Wyman, Sarah R. Wyman, Bill Russell, John Wade, Hannah Wade, John F. Harris, Phebe Harris, Edmun Parker, Thaddeus Parker.

Medford.—Anna Teel, Anna Briant, Leonard Bucknam, Anna Bucknam, Matilda Johnson.

Cragie's Point.—Elijah Wheeler.

Charlestown.—Stephen Symmes, Priscilla Symmes, John Swan, Samuel Gardner, Priscilla Reed, Charles Gordon, Ezra Welsh, Caleb Harrington, Sarah Gardner, Patience Gardner, Abigail Tufts, Caroline Griffin, Nathan Field, Jacob Page, John Tapley.

Cambridgeport.—E. F. Valentine, N. C. Valentine, Martha Valentine, Jane Valentine, Moses B. Houghton, Almira Houghton, Moses Ward, Ira Ward, Amos Hazeltine, Phebe Hazeltine, Susan Hazeltine.

Cambridge.—Josiah Johnson, Jonathan Hunt, Betsey Hunt, Ozias Morse, Sullivan B. Ball, William Hunnewell.

In comparing the Narrative of Miss R. with the Report of the Boston Committee, we ask those who may suppose they meet with any material contradiction, to bear in mind that there is one error pervading nearly the whole of that very able and forcible document. It is this—adopting as *facts* the exculpatory and laudatory statements regarding the Convent, made by the Superior and her Nuns, and the Bishop and his Priests. Thus, the Committee vouch for the propriety and tenderness of the penances imposed, of which they knew nothing; they assume a distinction between the Ursuline and other Nuns, which does not exist; declaring that they "are *openly* engaged in the most useful and elevated offices of humanity in *the presence of the world*," and that "their dwelling was accessible at proper times to the parents and friends of its numerous inmates." But how accessible? Did any Protestant parent or guardian ever see the *school room*, or the sleeping or eating rooms in which fifty of their daughters were taught, fed, and lodged? No. Was there ever any examination or public exercise of the scholars, which their parents were allowed to witness? None. Even Hon. S. P. P. Fay, who states in his testimony on the trial of Buzzell that he had had daughters in the Convent six years, and had visited it at all times, also declares on oath—"I never saw the school at the Convent, and never but once went beyond the parlor. When I wished to see my children, they were sent into the parlor, and when I wished to see any of the "Community," (their teachers,) saw them also in the parlor. The only time I went beyond the parlor, was *once* when I saw the ceremony of taking the white veil," (probably in the chapel.) Levi Thaxter, Esq. another highly intelligent Protestant patron of the Convent, testified that he was never in the school, though he went to the Convent very frequently. He saw his daughters in the parlor. When he wished to see any one they were sent for.

This, then, is the whole amount of "the dwelling being accessible at proper times to the parents and friends" of the pupils there. They were admitted to a common parlor, and not permitted to enter any other room in that spacious establishment. No *Protestant* eye ever saw the apartments of the Nuns, except on the occasion when the selectmen of Charlestown examined the building by appointment, the day of the riot. Even the physician, as we understand, never saw any of the *Religieuse*, to prescribe for them, in their private apartments. When sick, they were attended by the infirmarian, one of their own order.

An attempt to establish a Protestant school on such a plan of secrecy as this, would not be tolerated by judicious parents a moment. Are Catholic instructers of young ladies more entitled to confidence in these respects than Protestant teachers would be? Suppose a community of Episcopalian females should open a seminary for young ladies, and admit no person to go beyond a certain common visiting room. Suppose, that while they refused access to all other men or women, they freely admitted to their most private apartments, at all times of day or night, a number of clergymen, of their own denomination, by whom they were required to confess in private, without reserve, all their faults, wishes, and feelings. and submit to any penances these clergymen might impose on them, both sexes being under a solemn vow, which debarred them from ever marrying. Suppose one of the rules of the establishment was never to enter a room without first knocking three times, and waiting for the knocks to be returned. Would such an institution, so conducted by Protestants, be approved?

We ask a discreet and discerning community, to divest themselves of the false notion that the seminary at Mount Benedict was invested with a mysterious sanctity any more than our own colleges and schools. All the forms of Protestant worship are observed at Harvard college, but who thought of charging the young men with "sacrilege," and with intolerance to the Unitarian religion, when they committed riots, and depredations upon property there last summer, for which they were indicted? Even should our state be disgraced by a lawless mob burning down the University chapel, in the impulse of a blind fury, incited by vague rumors that a student, who had run away, and been carried back, had been put to death; who would think of attributing the deed to "the deep-seated repugnance to the" *Unitarian* "faith and form of worship which exists in every" *Orthodox* "community?" Who would call upon us, on this score, to lay aside our "*prejudices*" against Unitarianism?

Where is the distinction between the two cases? The Convent was either a religious establishment, for the worship of Roman Catholics, or it was a seminary of learning for the education of Protestant young ladies. If it were the former, it was no place for Protestant children. If it were the latter, then it is entitled to no sanctity; its "vessels" are no more "sacred," its "cross" is no more "holy," its "vestments" are no more "consecrated," than are the furniture and wardrobe of the teachers of a Protestant school. Surely it will not be pretended that a Nunnery in one room of a building can sanctify a school kept in another, by the Nuns themselves as teachers.

God forbid that we should say one word in extenuation of the outrage upon the Convent. It was every thing vile which a midnight attack upon the dwelling of defenceless females could be, where neither virtue nor life were sought or assailed; but we protest against the attempts that have been made in reports, in legal arguments, and even in judicial charges, to exaggerate this outrage, as "a scene of popular madness and of culpable official neglect, that can hardly find a parallel in that period of the French Revolution which will ever be remembered as the reign of terror." It was not an attack upon the religious worship of the Roman Catholics, and it did not have its origin in "a spirit of intolerance, fatal to the genius of our institutions." There are six hundred and forty Roman Catholic churches and mass houses in the United States, and who ever heard of religious worship in any of them being disturbed? No longer ago than the 26th of October, 1834, a splendid new Catholic cathedral at St. Louis, Missouri, was consecrated on SUNDAY, *amidst the discharging of cannon and the ringing of bells!* and later still, a Protestant senator of Ohio, standing in the streets of Cincinnati, was compelled to take his hat off, in honor to the Catholic ceremony of the passing *host.* Here in our own city of Boston, which we are striving so hard to brand with "intolerance," what religious society has ever enjoyed more privileges than have always been extended to the Catholics? Whose presses are more indulged in the full licentiousness of attack upon their religious opponents, than the two Catholic presses of Boston? One of them, the Catholic Sentinel, not a month ago, held the following excessively gross language, reflecting on the purity of the wives and daughters of all Protestant Christians who worship at the Methodist Episcopal Church. That paper of February the 7th, 1835, speaking of a young man who had been converted from the Catholic to the Protestant religion, says that "he is loved as an Adonis by these incontinent women and girls who go to the *assignation churches* to consecrate their hearts, not to God, but to the passion of illicit love."

Here is the real intolerance in this matter. The prevailing notion seems to be that true toleration requires Protestants to shut up their mouths and their presses against Catholics, but that the Catholics may say any thing they please against Protestants! Religious tolerance or intolerance has no more just connection with the destruction of the Catholic school at Mount Benedict, than it had with the riots last summer against anti-slavery societies in New York. Orthodox churches were destroyed by lawless mobs in those outrages, because anti-slavery lectures had been delivered in them; but who cried out religious intolerance then? Who thought that "the moving cause of such violence was deep-seated repugnance to the" *Orthodox* "faith and form of worship?" And yet this might have been assigned as the cause of those riots, with the same propriety a majority of a committee in the Massachusetts Legislature have recently declared that the moving cause of the destruction of the Ursuline Convent was "that deep-seated *repugnance* to the Catholic faith and form of worship, which exists in almost every Protestant community." That highly intelligent committee go farther, and really deprecate the existence of "strong *prejudices* against the peculiarities of that faith." "*Prejudice?*" Is our opposition to the "peculiarities" of Romish indulgences and auricular confessions a prejudice? Is our "repugnance" to the establishment in this country of the monastic institutions which Luther put down three hundred years ago, and which even Spain and other Catholic countries are beginning to abolish, a "prejudice?" If this be intolerance, then it would be intolerant to oppose in any form the "peculiarities" of the Inquisition, should it finally, after being driven out of Europe, take refuge in Massachusetts.

This cry of intolerance against ourselves, because a villainous mob have burnt down a Catholic school-house, is unjust to our own character and institutions, and ought to be arrested before it becomes stamped forever by the seal of history. The Propaganda of Rome, and the founders of the Leopold fund in Austria, to convert heretics in America, could not have found better missionaries for their purpose, than the scoundrels who burnt the Convent. Our own public acts and documents are at this moment quoted most effectually in the great West, by the Catholics, to excite sympathy for their religion, by representing it as terribly persecuted in this land of professed tolerance. It was the mistaken impulse of popular indignation, fomented by the elopement and mysterious return to the Convent of Miss Harrison, and by the indiscreet threats of the Superior to the selectmen of Charlestown, that "the Bishop has twenty thousand of the vilest Irishmen at his command, and there will be a retaliation; *you will have your houses torn down over your heads, and you may read your riot act till your throats are sore, and you'll not quell them.*"*—It was these "facts that contributed to the ex-

* Mr. Attorney-General Austin, in his eloquent argument against

citement which preceded the outrage, and led to its commission," and not, as we have permitted ourselves to be made to believe by the Catholics themselves, "a spirit of intolerance fatal to the genius of our institutions."†

What then is our duty as Christians and good citizens? To tell the truth, or to keep back the truth, for fear that "offences must come?" Are we not bound to bring this question back to its true position, as an outrage upon private property and personal right, an invasion of domestic security and the immunity of habitation, and an offence against public justice and public decency? Let us treat it as a *civil*, and not as a *religious* question, condemning it as strongly as if it were the destruction of a Protestant school-house by a lawless mob; and thus justly relieve ourselves of the mountain of odium we have been laboring to heap upon our institutions, as if there really had been a terrible "spirit of religious intolerance" toward the Roman Catholic worship "unexpectedly developed among us."

It does not follow that we must approve of the institution at Mount Benedict, because we abhor the act by which it was destroyed. We need not turn Catholics in order to prove that we are not intolerant Protestants. We are not obliged to unite with Romanists, in proclaiming our own religious intolerance, in order to show that we sympathize

---

Buzzell, says, in relation to this fact sworn to by Mr Edward Cutter:—"She (the Superior) is accused of having told Mr. Cutter that 'the Bishop had twenty thousand of the vilest Irishmen under his control,' and she acknowledges (much as such an acknowledgment might be supposed to operate against her) that she said so, or something to that effect"

† The origin of the mob has been ascribed, by the Superior herself, to the right cause. That lady, when under oath, testified, that while the Convent was in flames, "she told Mr. E. Cutter that it all originated from Miss Harrison going to his house." Judge Fay also testified, that he left his daughter in the Convent, and went home leaving a mob at the gate of the Convent, the night of the riot, satisfied that no violence would be attempted, because, knowing no cause for any other excitement but Miss Harrison leaving the Convent, and believing this was all explained, he did not feel alarmed. It did not occur to him that there was *any other cause* to produce such a result, (the riot) And yet, *five* months after, Judge Fay discovers and publishes the discovery, that Miss R was the whole cause of the mob. because she had said to his wife nearly two years ago, that she hoped to be an instrument of showing the truth!

with them for their loss of property by violence. We are not called upon to shut the door against all secessions from Catholic Nunneries, by lending our help to carry into effect against a Protestant daughter of one of our own citizens, the dogma of "mother church," that *whenever a Catholic changes his religion, his motives and conduct are to be invariably suspected, and his honesty never trusted.*"

No. We are bound to put forth all the vigilance and majesty of the laws to detect, and punish and redress this outrage upon the peace and dignity of the commonwealth; but we are not bound to deplore our "repugnance" to the Catholic religion as a disreputable "*prejudice*," and least of all are we called on to pronounce panegyrics upon Nunneries and Catholic seminaries, in order to indemnify the sufferers by inducing more Protestant Christians to neglect our own schools, and send their daughters to be educated in a Convent.

It is a question affecting *education*, and not affecting religious toleration; and it is time to correct the error that there is no distinction in matters of religious concernment between a Catholic Monastery and a Catholic Church; between a seminary for educating Protestant girls by Catholic teachers, and a purely religious Community of Catholics, exercising their forms of devotion without disturbing the public peace, or obstructing others in their religious worship. Neither should it be forgotten that the constitution, which declares that "all religious sects and denominations shall be equally under the protection of the law," also declares, that to be entitled to such protection, they must "demean themselves peaceably and as good *citizens* of the commonwealth."

In one word, and as a full justification of the present publication of these Suggestions and the accompanying Narrative; we ask, if females who are hereafter to become models of fashion in our most refined circles of society, and the future mothers of American citizens, are to be educated in Catholic Convents, is it not a matter of vital importance, that the interior discipline of such institutions should be fully made known? Our maxim is, "Prove all things, and hold fast that which is good."

NOTE.—The Boston Committee claim an exemption for Ursuline Convents from the "popular odium" which they admit is just against other Cloisters, on the ground that the former are devoted to education and works of charity. They can have read history to little purpose, if they do not know that the great argument in favor of all Monasteries, three hundred years ago, and since, was and ever has been, that they were seats of learning and hospitals of charity. Take the following from Rees' Cyclopædia.

"Although none in this enlightened period can approve either the original establishment or continued subsistence of Monasteries, yet the destruction of them was *felt* and *lamented*, for a considerable time, as a great *evil*. One inconvenience that attended their dissolution was the loss of many valuable books, for during the dark ages religious houses were the repositories of literature and science. Besides, they were *schools of education* and learning, for every Convent had one person or more appointed for this purpose, and *all the neighbors* that desired it *might have their children taught grammar and church music there, without any expense*. In the Nunneries, also, *young females were taught to work and read*, and not only people of the lower ranks, but most of the noblemen's and gentlemen's daughters *were instructed in those places*. All the Monasteries were also, in effect, great hospitals, and were most of them obliged to relieve many poor people every day. They were likewise houses of entertainment for all travellers. And the nobility and gentry not only provided for their old servants in these houses, but for their younger children and impoverished friends, by making them first monks and nuns, and in time priors and prioresses, abbots and abbesses."

It follows, therefore, that if the argument of the Boston Committee, in favor of establishing Ursuline Convents, is a good one, it is just as good for re-establishing the whole monastic system which the Reformation abolished, three hundred years ago. In fact it would seem as if the admirers of Catholic Cloisters in this country, really meant to set about seriously reforming back the Reformation!

SIX MONTHS IN A CONVENT.

In the summer of 1826, while passing the Nunnery on Mount Benedict, Charles town, Mass., in company with my school mates, the question was asked by a young lady, who I think was a Roman Catholic, how we should like to become Nuns. I replied, (after hearing her explanation of their motives for retirement, &c.) "I should like it well," and gave as my principal reasons, their apparent holy life, my love of seclusion, &c. The conversation which passed at that time made but little impression upon my mind. But soon after, the "*Religieuse*"* came from Boston

* By the term "*Religieuse*" I mean those who constituted the Ursuline Community.

to take possession of Mount Benedict as their new situation. We were in school, but had permission to look at them as they passed. One of the scholars remarked, that they were Roman Catho lics, and that our parents disapproved of their tenets. The young lady who before asked the question, how we should like to become Nuns, and whose name I have forgotten, was affected even to tears in consequence of what passed, and begged them to desist, saying, "they were saints; God's people; and the chosen few;" that "they secluded themselves that they might follow the Scriptures more perfectly, pray for the conversion of sinners, and instruct the ignorant* in the principles of religion." This conversation, with the solemn appearance of the Nuns, affected me very sensibly, owing probably to the peculiar state of my feelings. The impressions thus made re-

* By the word *ignorant* is meant what they term heretics.

mained on my mind several months; and at the age of thirteen years and four months I asked my parents if they were willing I should become an inmate of the convent. This proposition my parents were inclined to treat as visionary; but they soon discovered themselves to be in an error. Nothing of consequence was said upon the subject; but soon after, owing to the delicacy of my health, and other reasons, it was deemed expedient for me to visit my friends in New Hampshire, and being fond of retirement, this arrangement accorded very well with my feelings.

While in New Hampshire I spent many pleasant hours, which I think of with delight. Memory oft brings to view and faithfully delineates those hours of retirement and happiness which I imagined I should spend, were I an inhabitant of a cloister.

While writing this narrative, I often lament my little knowledge of history, for had I been more acquainted with it, I do not think I ever should have united myself to an institution of this nature. But to proceed; I never could prevail on my parents to say much on this subject. I kept silence, resolving in my own mind to become acquainted with some one who would introduce me to the Superior of the Ursuline Community, but did not ask any one till after the death of my mother. Previous to that event, I had become acquainted with Miss M. H., a domestic in Mr. H. J. K.'s family, near my father's house, in Charlestown.

After my mother's decease, while residing with my father, my sisters being absent, Miss H. came to our house and begged me to keep her as a domestic a little while, as she had no place. She had walked a great way for the purpose of seeing Mr. K., who had moved away. This was in the fall of 1830. After consulting with my father, I concluded to let her stay. She found me in great trouble and grief, in consequence of the absence of my two younger sisters, whom I very dearly loved, and who had gone to reside with my sisters in Boston. After family prayers were over, and I about retiring, I stepped from my room to see if Miss H. had extinguished her lamp, when, to my surprise, I found her kneeling and holding a string of beads. I asked her what she was doing. She did not speak for some time When she did, she said she was saying her "Hail Marys."* I asked her what the "Hail Marys" were, at the same time taking hold of the beads. She then said, "I say my prayers on these to the Blessed Virgin." My friends will of course excuse my curiosity at this time, for I had never before learned their manner of praying to saints and angels. Before I left her, she showed me an *Ag-*

---

* *Catholic Prayer, (translated from the Latin.)*—"Hail, Mary! full of grace; our Lord is with thee! Blessed art thou among women, and blessed is the fruit of thy womb, JESUS! Holy Mary, mother of God, pray for us, sinners, now and at the hour of our death. Amen."

nus Dei,* which she wore to preserve herself from the temptations of Satan. I cannot remember all the conversation which passed the next day on the subject, but I learned that she had been acquainted with the Nuns in Boston, and was also acquainted with the Superior.

The first pleasant day, I asked her to accompany me to the Superior, which she did, and appeared by her questions to know my motive. She introduced me to the Superior in the following manner. We were invited by a Lay Sister† to sit, who, after retiring, in a few moments made her appearance, requesting Miss H. to see her in another room. Soon after, the Superior came in and embraced me with much seeming affection, and put the following questions to me:—how long since the death of my mother; whether I ever attended the Catholic church, or

---

* Lamb of God;—a small piece of wax sewed up in silk in the form of a heart.

† Those Nuns who are occupied in domestic affairs.

knew any thing of the principles of their religion; what I had heard respecting them; of their order; my views of it; what progress I had made in my studies; whether I had attended much to history; knew any thing of embroidery, drawing, or painting, or any other ornamental work; whether I had ever assisted in domestic affairs. After which questions, taking my hand, she said, "O, it feels more like a pancake than any thing else."* She inquired in what capacity I desired to enter the institution, whether as a Recluse or a scholar; whether I had done attending school, &c. I replied that I did not consider my education complete; that I wished to go into the school attached to the Nunnery on the same terms as other pupils, until I had made suffi-

* This may appear laughable, but as I intend to publish all which will be for the benefit of the reader, I cannot refrain from mentioning this, in order to show the course of flattery, &c. made use of by the Superior and those connected with the establishment, to draw the inexperienced into their power, and make them converts to the religion of the Pope.

cient progress to take the veil and become a Recluse; that my father was averse to my becoming a *Nun*, but I was of opinion that he would concur with my Episcopal friends, in not objecting to my becoming a *pupil*. In the course of the interview, the Superior conversed much upon the Scriptures, and intimated that I ought to make any sacrifice, if necessary, to adopt the religion of the cross; repeating the words of our Saviour, "He that loveth father or mother more than me, is not worthy of me," &c.

At a subsequent interview the Superior desired me to see the Bishop, or clergy, remarking, she believed I had a vocation for a religious life, and the Bishop would tell me whether I had or not. She also asked if I was acquainted with a Catholic friend who would introduce me to the Bishop, and mentioned a Mr. R., who would introduce me to him. I was unacquainted with Mr. R., but had seen him at my sister's house in Boston. She said that the Bishop or Mr. R. would also discuss the matter with my father, and reconcile him to Catholicity. After consulting some friends who were in favor of the Catholic religion, I consented to see Mr. R.; who, being requested, called at my father's, gave me some scripture proofs of the infallibility of the Romish Church; as, "Thou art Peter, and upon this Rock I build my church, and the gates of hell shall not prevail against it;" and "whose sins ye retain they are retained, and whose sins ye remit they are remitted." "He that will not hear the church, let him be to thee as an heathen man and a publican." He (Mr. R.) desired I would secrete the paper upon which the texts were quoted. He then took his leave, saying he would call to see me in town soon at the Misses S., when he would introduce me to the Bishop.

I will here remark, that previous to my joining the Community, I heard of many miracles wrought by Catholic Priests. Mrs. G. brought a lady one day in a chaise to show me her eyes, which were restored by means of a Priest, Dr. O'F. She, as Mrs. G. stated, was totally blind, but having faith in miracles, she knelt to her confessor, requesting him to heal her. After touching her eyes with spittle and holy oil, she immediately "received her sight."

Before the next interview with the Su perior, I visited my Protestant friends, the Misses S., when Mr. R. called and proposed to introduce me to the Bishop. He accordingly accompanied me to the Bishop's, and introduced me as the young lady who wished to become acquainted with the tenets of the Church, and recommended to him by the Honored Mother the Superior, with directions for his ascertaining my vocation as a fit subject for a Recluse. The Bishop asked me if I knew the meaning of the word "Nun;" how long I had thought of becoming a Nun; my opinion, and the opinion of my friends, in regard to Catholicity. And as my feelings were easily wrought upon, more particularly at this time, questions were put to me, which more mature deliberation leads me to think were put under the impression that I was very ignorant, and which were very unpleasant for me to answer. He even went so far as to judge my secret thoughts, saying he knew what was then passing in my mind. I then took my leave, undecided what course to pursue, and very little edified by the conversation of the Rt. Rev. Bishop. The Bishop gave directions to Mr. R. to purchase a Catechism of the Catholic Church in the diocese of Boston, (published with the approbation of the Rt. Rev. Bishop Fenwick,) which I refused to accept.

About a week afterwards I called upon the Superior, and made her acquainted with my conversation with the Bishop; likewise with my refusal of the Catechism. On learning that my desire was still strong to become an inmate of the Convent, she smilingly said, that for one so young as I was, to wish to seclude myself from the world and live the life of a *Religieuse*, was impossible. I remarked I did not like the Bishop so well as I expected. She exclaimed, "O! he is one of the servants of God; he did so to try your vocation;" and said that I should like him the better the next time I saw him.* After recommending me to pray for grace, she caused me to kneel and receive her blessing; after which she embraced me, and I returned to my father's house. I shortly after visited the Misses H. in Charlestown, and was introduced to Mrs. G., who was acquainted with the tenets of the Catholic Church, and also with Mr. B., the Catholic Priest. After a short acquaintance with her I

* I did like him the next time that I called upon him, for he conversed in the most solemn manner, and after learning my name, said, "Is it possible that you have a saint's name!" and gave me St. Teresa, as my namesake, a beautiful wax figure, habited as an Ursuline Nun.

was requested to converse with Mr. B. the Priest, which I did, and liked him very much. He also supplied me with books, from which I learned that I ought to venerate and receive the religion of the Catholic Church as the *only one and true religion.*

On Good Friday evening, I heard the most affecting Catholic sermon,* in Charlestown, I ever listened to, upon the Passion of our divine Redeemer. I soon after visited at Mrs. G.'s, where I saw a fine drawing, exhibiting the peaceful and flourishing condition of the Holy and Apostolic Church, until the time of the Reformation under Martin Luther. Mrs. G. recounted the sufferings of the Catholic Church in consequence of this "pretended" reformation. My friends will understand, that by this time I had become a constant visiter at the Convent. On being sent for at one time by the Superior, I met the Bishop at the Convent,

* I had before attended the lectures in Boston, at the time of the controversy between Dr. Beecher and the Catholics.

who was playing with the dogs; at the same time the Superior hastily approaching, embraced me in the most affection ate manner; as she did ever afterwards when I visited her at the Convent. She introduced me to the Bishop again, who did not appear to recognise me, and said that I was sister to the lady who visited him in Boston. At this time I thought the Superior and Bishop the most angelic persons living, and in one instance gave way to anger in cousequence of hearing a few words spoken against them. On being told that my mind remained still the same, the Bishop remarked, "I will pray for you," and recommended to me the advantage of contінning under the instruction of the Priest, and said he should like to see my father or sister.

After the interview with the Bishop, I returned to my father's, who was much displeased with the steps I had taken, and bade me renounce all connection with the Catholics, or leave my friends. (This he said in a moment of excitement.) But, being so much attracted by the apparent holiness of the inmates of the Convent, and viewing this as the only true Church, I wished to become a member of it.

Perhaps it will be proper to state some of Mrs. G.'s conversation. After hearing from her a pleasing account of the life of a Nun, &c., I mentioned I should like to become one, and would, if I could prevail on my father and friends to consent; but unless I could, I must despair, as they would not be willing to advance the *money* which would be needed to go there. She replied, "It is not *money* that will ever induce them to take you; it must all be the work of God." She asked me what my Church friends* said upon the subject. On my telling her that they were reconciled to my entering the

* My friends of the Episcopal Church thought I could have the privilege of writing when I desired to see them.

institution, particularly as a scholar; that they liked the seclusion of the Convent, &c Mrs. G. stated she could see not the least objection to my following my own inclination. I then took my leave, promising to see her at my friend Mrs. H.'s. The next time I saw her, she advised me to leave my father's house and all, for the sake of Christ. She said she would procure me ornamental work, which would support me, independent of my relatives, &c., which she did. I thanked her most heartily, and told her I thought I should be happy, if I were certain of going to a Cloister. She gave me her word that I should. I then took up with her advice and left my friends, I thought for life, as I had no doubt but that I should soon enter the Convent, resolving to leave all for the love of God, and to consecrate the remainder of my days to his service I believed Mrs. G. to be my sincere friend, and an Episcopalian, as she had always told me she was, and placed myself under her protection.

After visiting some Protestant friends, I found means to procure my clothing, &c., and went immediately to reside opposite the Catholic church. I employed myself while there in doing ornamental work for my Catholic friends, and also in working lace for the Bishop, the altar, &c. About this time I was offered compensation, but refused it, and received a present of ten dollars, a crucifix, a pearl cross, and two books, with my name stamped upon them in gold letters, which presents I received as tokens of kindness and friendship.* And wishing to deny myself of any thing worldly, I gave up what jewelry I had, telling them I knew of no greater sacrifice I could at that time make, than to give up all the treasures my dear mother left me. I also gave my globe

* I wish to have it understood, that the lettering on these books was my new name, "Mary Agnes Teresa." My baptismal name, it will be recollected, is Rebecca Theresa. The books were given me by Mrs. G., who said they were from the Bishop; and he afterwards, in the Convent, confirmed the statement, saying, he knew at that time of my vocation, and for that reason sent me a religious name, which was a Saint's name.

and goldfish, which were a present to me. At that time I thought I was *holy*, and could hardly speak to a Protestant. I had read many Catholic books. My time was wholly employed in working for the Catholics, except my hours for meditation and prayers.

The ordinance of baptism* was administered to me by Mr. B., himself and a Mrs. P. standing sponsors for me; my former baptism being considered by the Catholics *invalid*. While in Charlestown, I stood sponsor for Mrs. G.'s daughter, of whom I shall speak in the course of this narrative. I would here remark, had I taken up with the advice given me by many of my friends, I should not now have the unpleasant duty of relating these facts; but so it was; I had imbibed a relish for what I supposed to be "real pleasures," but which, alas! I have found,

* At the time of my baptism, I was anointed with oil; a piece of salt was put in my mouth the Priest breathing three times upon me, and touching my eyes, ears, and nose with spittle, speaking Latin all the while. They profess to take these ceremonies from the Scriptures.

by sad experience. to be like the "waters of Marah." At an interview with the Superior, I was introduced to two of the "chosen Religieuse," the mother assistant and Mrs. Mary Benedict. The first question asked, was what word I brought from my friends. On my hesitating to give an answer, she insisted upon knowing what they said; on which I told her all they had said, word for word, as nearly as I could recollect; also the advice I received from a Mr. E., which appeared to displease her much; and although she strove to suppress her feelings, it was evident she was much displeased.

After some questions respecting Mr. E. the Superior remarked, he was none other than the man who made children's books. She also questioned me with regard to a conversation which took place between my brother and myself on Charlestown bridge, (which was published in the "JESUIT,"* highly exaggerated,) and ap-

* I afterwards asked Priest B. to explain what it meant; he

peared greatly pleased with the language of my brother, saying, with peculiar emphasis, "O, you will die a martyr to the cause of truth, should you die under persecution." I took my leave of her, promising to call again when she should desire.

After this, she wrote a letter to my father, of the contents of which I was then ignorant, but have since learned it contained offers of two or three quarters' schooling, free of expense. My father says he treated it with contempt; and his answer by the bearer was briefly this: "he wished me to have nothing to do with that institution; that my friends would prefer my going to a Protestant seminary." At my next interview with the Superior, she however told me, my father had become reconciled to my remaining with them two or three quarters; after which time, he would inform

---

said Dr. O'F. made a mistake in writing it for the press; and he promised it should be corrected. For the paragraph from the Jesuit, see Introduction.

them whether he could consent to have me stay there longer, as a teacher of music.* She previously presented me with some slate pongee, which was the uniform dress worn by the scholars in the public apartments; telling me at the same time to prepare myself and have my things ready by such a day. She asked me, if I should come without the consent of my Boston friends, if I supposed they would insert any thing in the public papers, or make any disturbance, or come there for me? to which I replied, I thought not. After preparing myself for a public reception, I visited the Superior, when she said, if I would place myself under her care from this time, she would protect me forever; and particularly from the persecution of the "heterodox;" and she

* I attended music, because the Superior desired it; and she assured me there was no need of assistance from my friends, even if my father had consented, for I could with my needle be of sufficient use to the Community to support myself without their assistance. She also told me I should study when I chose, and might have the privilege of coming into the Religieuse Community to recite to her.

looked to heaven above for her reward.* She then stated that the Bishop had concluded to receive me, not as a member of the public department, but as a "Novitiate," which would screen me from the questions of the Protestant scholars. She also added, that I should be received as the other Sisters were, and that we were to support ourselves by our talents and industry. The names of the Sisters were, Mrs. Mary Ursula,† Miss Mary Magda-

---

* I wish it to be understood, that, being influenced by the Superior and Mrs. G.'s advice, after hearing Romish preaching and reading their books, I went to board at Mrs. H.'s, opposite the Catholic church, where I employed my time in ornamental work; visited the Convent often, and informed myself as much as possible of a Recluse's life; lived as retired as the "Charity Sisters," except visiting some of my relatives three times, twice accompanied with Romish friends.

† Mrs. Mary Ursula came from New-Hampshire, and was received as *Choir Religieuse.* She was the eldest in the Gommunity; this I learned from the Superior, who often reprimanded her for saying many words in an uncouth, rustic manner, (such as *daoun* for *down*, &c.) telling her of her ignorance, &c. She never refused complying with the *rules*, but when reprimanded, would kneel at once, and kiss the floor. I often wished to ask if she was happy, but dared not speak (without permission) to her. Their proceedings appeared so strange, that I was in continual fear. The Novices frequently trembled when approaching "the mother," particularly at confession.

lene, Miss Mary Joseph, and Miss Mary Austin. The latter was both teacher and pupil. I answered that I should like those conditions best. She then desired me to kneel down and take the following obli gation· "I do, with the grace and assistance of Almighty God, renounce the world for ever, and place myself under your protection, from this day to consecrate myself to his honor and glory, in the house of God, and to do whatever obedience prescribes, and tell no one of this obligation but Mr. B., in confession." After this, the Superior summoned two of the "Choir Religieuse," who conducted me to the garden, where they left me to amuse myself. Presently the Superior joined me, wishing to know how I liked the garden, the flowers, &c. Observing a pocket album in my hand, she asked what I had hoarded up there; some worldly goods? She took it, and examining it, desired to know if I wished to keep some money I had in it, (fifteen dollars.) I replied no; as I was going to join them, I would intrust it to her care She also requested me to sing one tune; I complied, and sung "There's nothing true but Heaven." Her observation was, she should wish me to commence immediately with music. I then left the Convent, and attended the sacraments of confession and communion; and on Sabbath morning, August 5th, 1831, I was attended to the gate of the Convent by my friend, Mrs. G. I was shown into the public parlor by the Lay Sister, and was requested to kneel and continue my devotion, until the Superior made her appearance. She soon came, and made a sign for me to follow her. She led the way into a long room, darkened, at one end of which stood a large crucifix, made of bone, which I was afterwards informed was made of the bones of saints. The Superior told me, in a whisper, it was the time of silence. But after arranging my dress, she took from her toilet a religious garb, which she placed upon my head, and bade me kiss it, saying it had been blessed by the Bishop. She then pronounced a short Latin prayer, while I was kneeling, at the same time giving me her blessing. After this, she conducted me into another apartment, where was a stranger, whom she called a Postulant;* and giving me permission to speak, she left the room. A Lay Sister then entered the room with refreshment, after partaking which, we had permission to walk in one particular path in the garden. This stranger picked up a pear, and began to eat it, and invited me to do the same; which I declined, being acquainted with the rules of the Convent, which are very strict, as will be learned in the course of the narrative.. She did not regard the rules so strictly as the Superior required, who, being made ac quainted with her conversation by separately questioning us, sent her away, as

* Candidate for a Recluse.

she said, to another order;* but I now know that this was not the case.

To return to our walk in the garden; the bell rang, when we were immediately conducted to the Religieuse Choir; and here the Superior caused me to kneel three times, before I could suit her After the performances were over, which consisted of the office of adoration to the Blessed Virgin and prayers to the Saints, repeated in the Latin tongue, of which I knew nothing, we proceeded to the refectory, where we partook of our "portions." After saying Latin, we kneeled and kissed the floor, at a signal given by the Superior on her snuffbox. Before eating, one of the Religieuse said, "In nomine domini nostri Jesu Christe,"† all making the sign

* I believed she had gone to another order, and after returning to my Sisters, told them so, (together with my pastor,) that she was with the Sisters of Charity; when, to my surprise, she called upon me, said she had never thought of going to another order, and that the Superior had not done by her as she agreed.

† In the name of our Lord Jesus Christ. When opportunity offered, I asked the Superior to explain the meaning. She said, in

of the cross, and responding, "Amen." After receiving our portions, we performed several devotions, such as kissing the floor and repeating Latin, while the "Angelus" was ringing. We then went immediately to the "community." On entering this room, the "Novices" kneel and repeat the "Ave Maria,"* kiss the floor, and seat themselves for recreation, according to the rules given by the Superior, entitled, "Rules by the Reverend Mother." The following are the rules, which were inclosed in a gilt frame and suspended in the community; and it is

---

a very solemn manner, "You must not, my dear Sister, give way to *curiosity*. Do you not recollect it is against the *rules* for a Religieuse to do so?" I answered, "Yes, Mamère!" and complied at once, (by kissing the floor,) when she observed: "A Religieuse should never have a will of her own; as she grew in perfection in the order, she would understand what these words mean; it will be revealed to you when you are deserving." She taught me to believe that the "Office of the Blessed Virgin," (which was in Latin, and which we all repeated, without understanding it,) was none other than that chanted in heaven by the Saints, around the throne of the Almighty, and called the sweet communion of "All Saints."

* Hail Mary.

the duty of every Novice to read them, at least, once a week.

1. To rise on the appearance of the Superior.

2. When reprimanded, to kneel at once and kiss the floor, until the signal be given to rise.

3. When speaking *of* the Superior, to say our Mother; when speaking *to* her, and to the professed Choir Religieuse, Mamère; to say Sister, when speaking *to* the Novices; *of* them, Miss; and *of* the professed Choir, Mrs.; to say *our* or *ours*, instead of *my* or *mine*.

4. To say "Ave Maria" every time we enter the community.

5. Before entering any room, to give *three* knocks on the door, accompanied by some religious ejaculation, and wait until they are answered by three from within.

6. Not to lift our eyes while walking in the passage ways; also, never to *touch* each other's hands.

7. To stand while spoken to by the Bishop or Superior, and kneel while speaking to them; to speak in a particnlar tone.

8. If necessary to speak to the Superior during a time of silence, approach her kneeling, and speak in whispers.

9. Never to leave a room without permission, giving at the same time our reasons.

10. To rise and say the "Hour"* every time the clock strikes, except when the Bishop is present. who, if he wishes, makes the signal.

---

* "*The Hour.*—O sacred heart of Jesus! always united to the will of thy Father, grant that ours may be sweetly united in thine. Heart of Mary! an asylum in the land of our captivity, procure for us the happy liberty of the children of Jesus. May the souls of the faithful departed, through the merits of Christ and mercies of God, rest in peace. Amen."

The above is what is called *an Hour;* there is a different, though similar one, for each of the twenty-four hours in the day. They are written and placed in two gilt frames. over the mantlepiece; twelve over the heart of Mary in one, and twelve over the heart of Jesus in the other. Every time the clock strikes, the one whose turn it is to lecture rises and says one of them.

The following are the written "*Rules and Penances of our Holy Father, Saint Augustine*," together with those of Saint Ursula, as near as I can recollect They are read at the refectory table every week.

1. To kneel in the presence of the Bishop, until his signal to rise.

2. Never to gratify our appetites, except with his holiness the Bishop's or a Father Confessor's permission.

3. Never to approach or look out of the window of the Monastery.

4. To sprinkle our couches every night with holy water.

5. Not to make a noise in walking over the Monastery.

6. To wear sandals and haircloth; to inflict punishment upon ourselves with our girdles, in imitation of a Saint.

7. To sleep on a hard mattress or couch, with *one* coverlet.

8. To walk with pebbles in our shoes.

or walk kneeling until a wound is produced. Never to *touch any thing* without permission.

9. Never to gratify our curiosity, or excrcise our thoughts on any subject, without our spiritual director's knowledge and advice. Never to desire food or water between portions.

10. Every time, on leaving the community, to take holy water from the altar of the Blessed Virgin, and make the sign of the cross.

11. If a *Religieuse* persist in disobeying the Superior, she is to be brought before the Bishop of the diocese, and punished as he shall think proper. Never to smile except at recreation, nor even then contrary to religious decorum.

12. Should the honored Mother, the Superior, detect a *Religieuse* whose mind is occupied with worldly thoughts, or who is negligent in observing the rules of the Monastery, which are requisite and necessary to her perseverance and perfec-

tion in a religious life, she should immediately cause her to retire to her cell, where she could enter into a retreat.

I shall now continue my narrative of the remainder of the first day. At recreation, the Postulant and I had permission to embrace, in a new form, the *Religieuse*. After that they congratulated me on my success, saying they had ever prayed for me since they had heard of my vocation. The evening bell for the Latin office now rang, and we assembled at the choir, where we performed such ceremonies as I before named, until time of retiring. As we were strangers, the Superior conducted us to the infirmary, where other Novices were preparing to retire, and before leaving it, bade us not to rise until we had orders. Next morning being holy day morning, the bell rang at three, instead of four, as it usually does, for meditation in the choir. While the *Angelus** was

* The Angelus is the bell rung while repeating the three salutations and three Hail Marys.

ringing, at five A. M., we were called to attend Complin and Prime, until half-past six; then Litany to the Saints. After Litany, the bell rang for diet in the refectory, every morning, except Friday; on which day we assembled for confession to the Superior.

The manner of confession to the Superior is as follows: the room is first darkened, and one lighted wax taper placed upon the Superior's throne; and she is considered as filling the place or station of the Blessed Virgin. After taking their places in the greatest order and silence, the Religieuse respond. Then the lecturess reads from a book, called Rules for the Ursuline Order, by Saint Ursula, about complaining of the cold, our clothing, food, &c. &c. They sit on their feet during the reading, a posture *extremely painful.* The reading finished, the Superior whispers to the Sisters to approach her separately, which they do; each one in her turn approaches, and repeats the following: "Our Mother, we acknowledge that we have been guilty of breaking the rules of our *Holy Order*, by lifting our eyes while walking in the passage-ways; in neglecting to take holy water on entering the community and choir; failing in respect to our Superior, and veneration to our Father; failing in religious decorum, and in respect to our vows,—poverty and obedience; for which we most humbly ask pardon of God, penance and forgiveness of you, our Holy Mother." As each one finishes, the "Holy Mother" gives her advice and penances, and her blessing; they then kiss her feet, and sometimes make the cross with their tongues on the floor; then making their inclination, they retire to the choir to perform the penances.

After they are all assembled in the choir, the Superior says, *Kyrie eleison*, and they all answer, *Kyrie eleison*; the Superior says, *Christe eleison*, and they answer, *Christe eleison*, &c. &c. She then says Litany to the Saints in Latin, beginning with "Sancta Maria," and they respond, "Ora pro nobis," &c. &c. This ceremony is very solemn. It is performed until eight o'clock, A. M., when we receive our portion, sitting on the floor. The bell rings at half-past eight for young ladies' recreation. Then we attend to study until a quarter before eleven; then private lecture until eleven; then bell rings for the examination of conscience till a quarter past eleven; then for diet. The services at diet* are, after repeating

---

* Our diet consisted of the plainest kind of food, principally vegetables and vegetable soups, Indian-puddings, and, very seldom, meat. Our tea was made of herbs, sometimes of the bitterest kind. We partook of this diet in imitation of the Holy Fathers of the Desert, to mortify our appetites. Pumpkins, stewed with molasses and water, served us sometimes as a dessert. Occasionally, we had mouldy bread to eat. A very insignificant piece of butter was sometimes placed on our plates. The Superior's diet was far better than ours; sometimes it was sumptuous, wine not excepted. I ascertained this, as I occasionally, in turn, went round to gather the fragments. She sent me, on two occasions, some apple parings to eat, as a part of my portion. Sometimes the Religieuse deny themselves any diet; prostrate, kiss the feet of those who remain at table, performing various kinds of penance, while the others are eating and listening to the reading. Those who have permission to deny themselves in the morning, take their work-baskets as they pass to the refectory; where they sew by candle-light, as the lecturess is reading. This has a solemn and impressive appearance.

Latin :—first, they seat themselves in order upon a bench, first crossing themselves in their appointed places, on one side of a long, narrow table; before each one lies a small linen napkin or servet, rolled around another small cloth, containing a knife and fork; beside each servet is a plate containing the "portion;" then the Superior enters and passes along to her table, at the head of the room, the Nuns making their inclinations as she passes. She then makes a signal on her snuff box, and the "Religieuse," whose turn it is to speak, says, "*Benedicite;*" the Superior answers, "*Benedicite;*" and so it continues, in a similar manner, from one to the other, the "Efficient"* repeating a Latin prayer. The Superior then makes the signal for the lecturess to read from the Lives of the Saints and Martyrs, while the others are eating. When the signal is given, each one rolls up the knife and fork in the napkin, and

* The Efficient is one who repeats prayers and officiates during the office and serves at Mass.

lays it as she found it; (they also open it at a signal;) and the one whose turn it is to do so, after kissing the floor, as a token of humility, takes from the drawer a white apron and a basket containing a napkin, and after putting on the apron, brushes the fragments from the tables into the basket, and takes the servets, making her inclination to each one. She then takes the articles off the Superior's table, one by one in a napkin, in a solemn manner. If any eatables fall on the floor, they must be taken up in a napkin, and not by any means with the bare hands.

After this the Superior makes a signal, and the lecturess and before-mentioned *Religieuse* kneel in the middle of the floor and kiss it, and immediately rise and join the others in repeating the Latin prayers; after which the lecturess rings the An gelus. During this ringing, they all kneel and repeat it, then assemble in the community for "recreation." During this they are permitted to converse with one another, but in a particular and low tone, and only on such subjects as the Superior shall give them; if she be absent, the conversation is usually on the subject last read at the table; and they work during the time. After recreation, public* lectures take place, and at one o'clock the bell rings for "visitation" to the altar, which, with the Vespers, occupy us an hour and a half. Then the Rosary is said. On hearing the bell again, we all assemble in the community, where there is a "point of prayer" read. Then lessons occupy us until five; meditation and reflection half an hour longer; then the bell again rings for diet, where we go through the observances before named; then recreation forty-five minutes; then the *miserere*, during which the bell rings; then public prayers in the choir: then the *Benedictus* rings, and the Lay Sisters†

* Public lecture means a subject read aloud by the lecturess.

† One Lay Sister remains kneeling in the entry until we get to the psalm called Te Deum, when she rings while we are saying it. The Religieuse bow or kneel, &c., but do not join in saying the office.

come up into the choir. Matins, lauds, and prayers continue from seven until nine o clock, when we retire while the bell is ringing, except those who attend lessons and penances. This concludes a day and its services. The same course was pursued every day except Fridays and Sundays, when there was some variation.

I had become, in about a week, apparently so great a favorite of the Superior, that although remiss in duties, it was in a measure overlooked. She would even reprimand the Religieuse for my example and my faults; one instance of which I will give. Failing to arrange the Superior's toilet and seat and cricket, it being my turn, one of the Religieuse was reprimanded in my stead, and immediately knelt and kissed the floor. After this I was sent for to the Bishop's room, where the young ladies assemble on Mass morning, and after kneeling, &c., the Superior asked me how things appeared; if they appeared as I thought they would; if I liked my food, &c. Feeling a repugnance to answer her, she said, "Recollect yourself." I told her I liked all pretty well, except my couch. She left, telling me to beg the intercession of Saint Teresa. The next day my couch was exchanged for a better, and the image of Saint Teresa put near it, for my use.

Soon after I became an inmate of the Convent, the Bishop came into the community, and said, "How does that little Nun? And what have you done with Sister Stimson?" The Superior answered, that she was not fit for the order, and she had sent her on to the Sisters of Charity. (See note on page 74.) He then, address ing me, asked how I liked Mount Bene dict. I said, "Very well, my Lord." He then said, "O, but you will have to strive with the temptations between the good and evil spirits;" and he then explained all the horrors of Satan; and asked me where Saint Teresa, my namesake, was; and if I had read her life; and told me to say, as she did, these words, "Now come, all of you; I, being a true servant of God, will see what you can do against me," by way of challenge to the evil ones; and beg her intercession. He told me my sister had been to see if I had taken the veil, or had any thought of taking it; and he said I might rest contented, as my friends would trouble me no more.* He then told me the difference between a holy life and a worldly life; said the Devil would assail me, as he did Saint Teresa, and make me think I ought to go back to the world; and make me offers of worldly pleasures, and promise me happiness. In order to prevent this, I must watch and pray all the time, and banish entirely worldly thoughts from my mind; and throw holy water at the evil spirits, and challenge them to come if they dare. Perceiving the unpleasant effect this had

* I have since learned it was my sister and another lady. They say he told them I had not taken the veil, but hoped I soon would do it.

on my feelings, he portrayed in lively colors the happiness which would flow from my resisting the evil spirits, and what a crown of glory would be placed on my head by the angels.

According to my Confessor's orders, I took upon myself many austere penances, &c.; but the Superior, noticing my exhaustion from this cause, released me from the austerities for a time, saying I was a favored one; and she gave me permission to rest, while the others rose to say *midnight matins** and hear Mass. On the exaltation of the holy cross, the Bishop gave us his blessing, we all kneeling in the community. In conversation with the Sisters, he remarked one had not a very pleasant countenance; and he asked me how I was pleased with my teacher, saying he hoped she put a more pleasant countenance on while instructing me.

* Midnight mass and midnight matins are said at night during Lent, and midnight mass always on Christmas. This is a time of special humiliation and prayer.

Once, while walking with the Bishop and Superior, we met a stranger, upon which the Superior required us to turn our backs while she conversed with him. After he left the garden, the Bishop and Superior held some conversation together apart from us, of which I overheard the following words of the Bishop: "I fear he did not come here accidentally, as he stated, but for some particular purpose." Immediately the Mother Assistant came to me, saying that gentleman looked very much like me, and asked me if he was not my brother; and having permission to look, I answered, "No, he is not." We then retired within the Convent. The Bishop observed to me just before we went in, that that gentleman looked no more like me than one of the dogs of the Convent.

I was particularly hurt in witnessing the austerities put on a Religieuse, named Sister Mary Magdalene, who came from Ireland. Once, while reciting the office, she, by accident or losing breath, spoke in a lower key than she should; at a signal from the Superior, she fell prostrate before her desk, and remained so for one hour, until the office was finished, when she had permission to rise. This was the first time I thought the Superior had done wrong.* Soon after this, in private confession to the Superior, she appeared determined to know my thoughts, and put many questions to me that were hard to answer. I would here remark, that this is the practice at auricular confessions. She told me to beg the intercession of my patron Saint, of the Blessed Virgin, and Saint Ursula. I complained to her of my strength's failing, and of my diet, not being such as I was used to; she replied, that a Religieuse should have no *choice*, and that I should have left my feelings in the world; and she immediately

* The Superior often made mistakes in repeating the office, by endeavoring to repeat it without the book. And I learned afterwards from Mary Francis that the Superior did not understand it.

imposed the following penances:—to make the sign of the cross on the floor with my tongue, and to eat a *crust* of bread in the morning for my portion. The first of these penances I did not fulfil to the letter, making the sign of the cross with my hand instead of my tongue.*

After this a daughter of my friend Mrs. G. came to the Convent, and was permitted to spend some time with me in private. I also had some trifles given me as presents for this little girl, and leave to send what word I wished to my friends. This girl told me at the time, she was coming there to school soon; I therefore sent by her my love to my friends, informing them that I liked the Convent very well, and should be very happy to see them, if they would not speak against my religion.†

* I would state to the reader, that those things were received on my part with great repugnance; but the Superior said they were to prove my vocation, and I submitted without a murmur.

† This message my friends never received, as I have since learned. I was deceived in regard to the friendship of Mrs. G,

Soon preparations were made for my taking the *vows* of a Religieuse, a Novena (nine days' devotion) being said for me, and for my perfection in a religious life, and prayers for the conversion of my friends. About this time my sponsor, the Priest, visited the Convent, and talked, as I then thought, like a godlike person. My reception was to take place *privately*, because we wished to keep my father ignorant of the manner in which I had been received; and because he might hear of it, should it take place publicly; as he had before said, I was not eighteen, and he could prevent my going there. They said he could not prevent me, as I was now of age. I was perfectly happy at this time, and presented the Superior with some lines of poetry, which gave her proof of my sincerity and contentment.

She appeared very much pleased with the verses, embraced me very affectionately, and expressed her hearty approbation of my perseverance in performing the duties of the order, and said the request for her entreaties that I might persevere in a religious life should be granted, and she would show the lines to the Bishop. She accordingly did so, when he was present one day, and he said he must write my conversion, for it was so much like Saint Teresa's, my namesake. After this she gave orders to have all my worldly dresses, being ten in number, and other articles of wearing apparel, altered for those young ladies whom she clothed and educated; and for me she ordered a long habit to be prepared, which was to be blessed by the Bishop; also a veil, which they said denoted purity and innocence.

One time I failed in rising at the Angelus,* which was not noticed by the Superior. The next morning a Religieuse did not rise until the ringing of the Angelus, and when she came into the refectory

* My time was to rise at the Angelus, which was rung at five, while the Religieuse rose at four, except on holy-day mornings, when they rose at three.

we were at diet. She brought her pillow, and kneeling, kissed it, and said as follows:—"I have neglected to obey the commands of the Superior, and have not risen until the Angelus, which I am most heartily sorry for; and I humbly ask pardon of God and penances of you, our Holy Mother." The Superior said no one who disobeyed her commands should be permitted to remain in this Monastery. Her penance was to kiss the floor and remain kneeling until lecture and diet were over.

The Bishop, about this time, came to examine our work, &c. After hearing us sing, he complimented us, said he should hardly have thought that I could have learned of heretics to sing and work so well; and desired me to learn him to work lace, as he feared I should not finish his *robe* for Christmas. After being presented, as usual, with wine, he retired. The Bishop's wine is presented in a golden cup. The Religieuse who presents it remains kneeling until he has drank it.

As was usual on Saturday evening, after signifying our obedience to the Superior, by prostrating and kissing the floor, we received permission to visit the "*sanctum sanctorum*" on Sabbath morning, to receive the eucharist, all of us except my teacher, (the one who the Bishop said did not look pleasant, and whom I saw in tears on Sunday morning.) The Superior made a signal for me to follow her into the Bishop's room, when, first inquiring into my feelings, as she usually did, she asked me what I thought of my teacher; if she had put any questions to me while at my lessons; and how long before I thought I should be able to pronounce my vows, and take charge of a class in music. She asked me, at another time, what I thought was the reason of my teacher's crying; (her name was Miss Mary Francis.) I replied I did not know. She said it was the operation of the Holy

Spirit, and her devotional feelings were very deep.

The next day, while we were at our recreations, Miss Mary Francis appeared in great distress from some cause, and in tears. She soon after pencilled a few lines, and approached the Superior kneeling, &c., and presenting the paper; she appeared confused and very angry, and bade her take a seat. After this the Superior thought it necessary for me to retire to the infirmary and take an emetic, which I did the next day. The day after this I had orders to take medicine, which I was averse to, and on my declining, the infirmarian* made the sign of the cross a number of times, and told me it was the Superior's orders, and I could not avoid taking a part of it. I remained in the infirmary two days without a fire, and the weather was very cold. I had then

* The infirmarian is one who tends upon the sick. I was as well as usual when I took the emetic.

permission to go to the choir, where I immediately fainted, at which the Superior was angry, and said in a whisper she had told me *I ought not to have any feelings.*

For a while Sister Mary Francis was not present at the office and recreations as usual, and the Superior gave as a reason for her absence that she was ill. But it will be necessary for me to leave for a moment Miss Mary Francis, and speak of Miss Mary Magdalene. The latter was put over me as a teacher in the room of Mary Francis, whom I then supposed to be sick; but I afterwards learned that she was confined, that she might have a better opportunity to clear herself of the temptations of Satan. Sister Mary Magdalene told me she was about to leave this world, and wished to give me some advice. She said she thought it was God's will to take her to himself. After reminding me of the respect due to the Superior, and of my negligence in not kissing the floor in the choir, and of my looking up while walking in the passages, she then spake of Sister Mary Francis; said she would soon be able to give me lessons as before; but wished to know which of the Novices I thought had the best vocation for a religious life, and which one would be most likely to return to the world. To the latter I replied, "Sister Mary Francis." She asked why. I said she did not appear to observe the rules so strictly as the others. She asked me if that would be any inducement for me. I replied, "No, not that." She appeared unable to talk, but notwithstanding her weak state and trembling hands, she sewed all the time. I told her it gave me pain to see her distress herself so. With a peculiar emphasis she said, "Sister, *obedience!*" and in a very affecting manner made the sign of the cross.

While at my lessons one day, in the hours of silence, the Superior and Mother Assistant came, wishing me to tell them where Miss Mary Francis was. I replied I had not seen her. They left the room, and soon Miss Mary Francis entered, in tears. The Superior followed, and seizing her by the arm, shook her violently, threatening to punish her for disobedience, and wished she had a *cell austere enough* to put her in, and exclaimed, "Shame! shame! you 'disedify' Miss Mary Agnes."* She then told her not to feign sickness again, but to show by her appetite her illness. After the penance of kissing the floor, &c, she gave her a number of prayers to copy for the Protestant scholars. And from that time we were watched with the strictest scrutiny. The next day the Superior gave me permission to write to my father. She said Miss Mary Francis was crazy, and she should not keep her in the Convent more than a month longer, if she did not reform.

---

* All the Nuns have the name of Mary, and added to it is the name of some canonized Saint. Miss Mary Agnes was my name.

Mary Francis' grief will be well recollected by those in the public apartments. The next day I wrote to my father. The letter* was corrected by Miss Mary Francis, who was not crazed, as stated by the Superior. I then whispered to her, (it being the time of silence,) and asked the cause of her grief. She wrote on a slate, "she could not." A Religieuse was in the room, watching us very narrowly, and to mislead the Religieuse, she reminded me of making false syntax. We next met in the community for recreation. The Superior gave the Mother Assistant permission to speak; (Miss Mary Francis was absent.) She began by asking how she did. The Superior answered, "She goes on in her old way;" and observed that she was unfit for the order. The Mother Assistant said, "O, Mamère, let me pray, at least, a month longer for her;" and turning to the No-

* This letter was never received by my father,

vices, asked them to join with her. The Superior granted her permission, but handed her a letter to read. The Mother Assistant, turning to us, said, "Sisters, pay attention This letter is from Miss Mary Francis' aunt, Miss I., of New York." The substance of it was, that she had received her (the Superior's) letter, and was sorry to have recommended to her that person, but she thought she had reformed, and would be a suitable member for a Monastery; and she begged pardon for introducing one to her who had disturbed the peace of her little Community, and hoped if it were possible she would not long be troubled with her, &c. The Superior said, after the close of the letter, "Sisters, you may still continue to pray for her, and I will see about this thing, as it may be a temptation of the adversary." Two or three days after this, I met Miss Mary Francis at my lessons in the community, and again asked her to tell me her distress by writing on the slate, or I would tell the Superior I could not learn of her. She begged I would not, and told me she was under a solemn obligation not to make known the cause of her grief. She asked me if I was happy; I told her I was not to see her unhappy, and again entreated her to tell me the cause of her tears. She said I must not tempt her to break her promise, for if we were detected in conversation, she would be made still more unhappy. I then asked, if she had recovered from her illness, why she did not go to her class, &c. Shesaid the Superior had forbidden her, but she could not answer any other questions. I had formed a strong attachment for this lady, and it gave me pain to see her so distressed.

At next recreation, the Superior sent us word to meet the Bishop in the medi tation garden. Sister Mary Magdalene being too exhausted to walk as fast as we did, the Bishop asked who that was, and being told, he burst into a laugh, and said, "Sister Magdalene, when are you going to heaven?" She replied, in a voice scarcely audible, "I have no will of my own, my Lord; whenever it shall please God to take me."* She thought she should not live to see Christmas. We then assembled in the community, and when all were seated, the Bishop inquired, "Where is that sober-faced Nun?" Being told by the Mother Assistant that she was giving lessons to Miss F., he took the letter before spoken of, and looking it over, handed it to the Mother Assistant, saying, "Why do you keep her, and why does she not go to her class?" The Superior said the young ladies were not pleased with her as a teacher. He asked if all disliked her. Miss Mary Benedict replied, "No, my Lord; some in the French class appear to like her;" on which he said, "Show them that letter."

At my next lesson, I told Mary Francis

---

* It is here to be understood, that Sister Mary Magdalene was in a consumption, and had entered the Convent nine months before in perfect health. She was worn out with austerities.

if she did not explain to me the cause of her grief I should certainly tell the Superior; for I could receive no benefit from her instructions while she was so confused, and the Superior had reprimanded me for not learning my lessons; and I promised if she would tell me I would not inform the Superior. She replied that she could not answer me *then*, but would think of it, and give me an answer in the afternoon. Accordingly, in the afternoon, a Religieuse being present, watching us, she communicated what I desired to know by writing on a slate,* and desired to know if I was happy. I answered that I did not like the Superior so well as formerly. She then wrote, that while at prayer and meditation she concluded it was her duty, particularly as I was dissatisfied, to give me some advice, and considered her promise before made as not binding; and receiving from me a

* We were at the piano; she pretended to write notes, &c.

promise of secrecy, she proceeded to say that she hoped she should be pardoned if any thing wrong was said by her, as my whole happiness depended on the words she should communicate. "I am," says she, "kept here by the Superior, through selfish motives, as a teacher, under a slavish fear and against my will. I have written several letters to my father, and have received no satisfactory answer; and I have for a long time felt dissatisfied with my situation. The Superior has failed in fulfilling her promise, not complying with the conditions on which I was received; which were, that as she was in need of a teacher, particularly in French and music, I might take the white veil, and leave whenever I chose; and my taking the veil, "as it was only a custom," should not compel me; and that my obligations should not be binding. My father thinks I can leave at any time, for I do not believe he has received my letters, and that letter you have heard read as

Miss I.'s is a forged one." We were here interrupted by the entrance of the Superior, who made a sign for me to follow her into the Bishop's room. After asking me how I progressed in my lessons, and hearing me read in the "Novices' Directory,"* she ob served that I looked melancholy, and commanded me to tell her the reason. I replied that I did not feel well, that my lungs were sore since taking the emetic,† &c. She said that was only a notion, and bade me tell the true reason without any more equivocation. My words were, I did not love her so well then as formerly. She ex claimed, "O, my child, I admire you for

* This is a book which is used only in Convents. It directs us to respect the Bishop as a representative of the person of Christ, and in confession as Christ himself; and the Superior as fulfilling the office of Mother of God.

† My lungs were also very sore in consequence of repeating the offices: so much so, that when present at recreation, when I had permission to speak, it gave me pain rather than pleasure. I have, since leaving the Convent, consulted several physicians, who have expressed it as their opinion, that the cause of my bleeding at the lungs, which frequently occurs, was originally the repeating the office and other services, in *one long, drawling tone,* which any one can know by trying to be very difficult.

your simplicity;" and asked me my reason for not loving her, which I declined giving. She commanded "*obedience*" with seeming mildness, and I told her that I thought she did not pay that attention to me she had promised, and that she was not so kind as formerly. She then said a Religieuse should have no will of her own; that their Superior put many things upon them, in order to try their vocation. She then recounted the sufferings of a certain Saint, and bid me pray to that Saint for protection; and showed me a phial, which she said contained some of Saint Teresa's tears; and said if I would save my tears while in devotion, she could tell by them whether I should ever arrive to the perfection of a Saint. She then gave me her blessing, and reminded me of my reception, which was soon to take place.

At my lesson in the afternoon I again conversed with Mary Francis concerning the letter, and requested her to inform me how my happiness was concerned. She said still that the letter read to the Community was a forged one; that Mrs. I. was her aunt and sincere friend; and did her father know her sufferings, and the treatment she received from the Superior, he would prosecute her; that she feared the Superior as she did a serpent. She then advised me not to bind myself, after my three months' "test or trial,"* to *that* order, by complying with the rules of "reception," any farther than would leave me at liberty to go to another if I chose; and I must not think, because they were wicked, that the inmates of all Convents were so. I assured her that although I had thought there were none good but Catholics, I now believed there were good and bad among all sects. She then requested me not to betray her, and told me the Superior intended to keep me

* When persons *first* enter the Convent, they take an obligation that they will spend the remainder of their days as a Recluse, but they are put on a three months' "test" or trial, to see if they have a "vocation" for that particular order; if not, they are generally placed in another.

there for life, and she thought it her duty to warn me of the snares laid for me. She disliked that order,* and wished me to inform her why, and in what manner I had come there. I related to her then, and during the next afternoon, all the particulars. She appeared very much surprised to learn that my friends had been opposed to my coming, as the Superior had told her that they had put me there for life. She said she had been taken from the public apartment, because she had been seen weeping by the young ladies; that should the Superior refuse to let her go, she should if possible make her escape; and named a Religieuse (Miss Mary Angela) who had made her escape before. She desired me, if she should be so fortunate as to make her escape, to ask, in private confession, permission to see my friends,

---

* Miss Mary Francis was educated, I believe, in the Convent of Saint Joseph, Emmetsburg; also known as the order of the "Sisters of Charity." She possessed an amiable disposition and superior talents, and was universally admired by the inmates of the school; and so far as my acquaintance went, she was deserving the esteem of every one.

and consult them about going to the "Sisters of Charity;" and if they were willing that I should go, she would procure me a situation, and by letter inform me of it. She was in great distress on account of *that* letter, which plainly unfolded the motives of the Superior. She said she should appear as calm as possible, as it was the only way to blind the eyes of the Superior, and enable her to escape; and requested me to give her all the information respecting the Superior's intentions that I could learn, and to listen to her and the Mother Assistant's conversation at recreation hours.

At recreation the Superior observed that Miss Mary Francis had no vocation for a religious life, as she had *refused* to attend the offices and prayers. At our next interview, I inquired of Mary Francis if she had *refused* to attend prayers; she replied no; that the Superior had discovered her intention to escape, and had *forbidden* her attending offices, communion, and confession, for exposing her feelings before the Religieuse; and that the Superior had imposed penance upon her, forbidding her to walk in the garden during recreation; and that the presents given her by the young ladies had been, with the Superior's permission, taken by some one from her desk. She remarked that we were exhorted to love and pray for those who spitefully use us, but she could not love the Community generally, they exercised so much cruelty towards her; that the treatment she received was for no other reason than because she had given way to tears, which were a great relief to her; she was happy, she said, to find one who sympathized with her, and who would not treat her with contempt, as the others did. She said also that the Superior had done wrong respecting her apparel.

I have now come to that part of my narrative in which I must again speak of the sufferings of Sister Magdalene.

One day she came from the refectory, and being so much exhausted as to be hardly able to ascend the stairs, I offered to assist her, and the Superior reprimanded me for it, saying her weakness was feigned, and that my *pity* was false pity. She then said to Sister Magdalene, (after we were seated,) in a tone of displeasure, if she did not make herself of use to the "Community," she would send her back to Ireland; on which Sister Mary Magdalene rose and said, "Mamère, I would like—"* The Superior cut short what she was going to say by stamping upon the floor, and demanding who gave her permission to speak, imposed on her the penance of kissing the floor. The Superior after this imposed hardships which she was hardly able to sustain, frequently reminding her that she had but a short time to work out her salvation, and that she must do better if she did not wish to suffer in purgatory.

* This, and other like half-uttered expressions, convinced me that she wished to return to her friends.

The Superior questioned me about my feelings; wished to know why I looked so solemn. I told her I was ill from want of *exercise*, that I was not accustomed to their mode of living, &c. She said I must mention it to my Confessor, which I did. The next time the Bishop visited us, he was in unusually high spirits, and very sociable; and he related several stories, which are not worthy of notice in this place. He again asked Sister Magdalene when she thought of going to that happy place, to receive her crown of glory. She replied, "Before the celebration of our divine Redeemer's birth, my Lord." He said she ought to be very thankful that she was called so soon.

I will here relate a conversation of the Bishop with the Superior at recreation hour, respecting the Pope, &c. After talking a while in French, he said he had received a long letter from the Pope, in which his Holiness congratulated him for his success in establishing the true religion in the United States, and made him offers of money to advance the interest of the Catholic Church, and more firmly establish it in America, &c. The Bishop then spoke of the Orthodox in Boston, and said Dr. B. had got himself in a "hornets' nest," from which he could not extricate himself. The Superior named a sermon delivered in the North Church by an Episcopalian, and said they must look out or *they* would get themselves into a "hornets nest." The Bishop mentioned a visit of Dr. O'F. at Dr. B.'s, and said Dr. O'F. had scarcely an opportunity to say a word, on account of the noise and crying of the children which were in the room, and with which Dr. B. was playing; said he appeared more engaged with the children than with the subjects of religion, &c. &c Miss Mary John, the Mother Assistant, exclaimed, "Is it possible, my Lord, that a man of God is treated in such a way by heretics?" "Yes," said the Bishop, "none but he that is unmarried careth for the things that belong to the Lord, how he may please the Lord: but he that is married careth for the things that are of the world, how he may please his wife." The Superior said Dr. B. possessed very little sense, and had a weak mind. The Bishop said that the doctor by the course he had taken, had made many converts to Catholicism; "And perhaps," said the Superior, "he is a wicked instrument in the hands of God to bring about good."

At another time, while walking on the Convent grounds, a cannon ball was picked up by one of the Religieuse, and the Bishop taking it, observed, as he gave it to the Superior, "Here is a British ball that has killed many a Yankee;" and he also made several other similar observations. At another time the Superior told the Bishop that two ladies met near the Convent; the words she used were, "One Yankee met another, and said, 'I *guess* you are a going to *independence*.' 'I *guess* I be,' said the other.' They then laughed heartily about it, and gave us permission to hold our recreation upon it. The Bishop remarked, the Yankees celebrated independence day in honor of *men*, and *appointed* days of thanksgiving, instead of celebrating the birthday of the Re deemer, in honor of God, &c.*

When I was again summoned to the Superior, she inquired as usual into the state of my feelings; and when I said I desired to see my friends, she replied, "Why, my dear Agnes, do you wish to see *worldly* friends? Who do you call your friends? Am not I your friend? Is not the Bishop your friend? If your worldly friends wished to see you, would they not

* We all had permission at one time to walk with the Superior in the meditation garden. The Superior heard a noise behind the fence, and sent her servants to learn the cause; they returned, informing her that two men were looking through the fence. The Superior remarked, the Bishop had said there was great danger to be apprehended from such persons; that if Protestants were to offer any violence to them, the judgments of heaven would fall upon the wicked; and God had founded them upon a rock so firm that it could not fall. The Superior gave orders to the porters not to allow strangers to walk over the grounds without her or the Bishop's permission.

come and see you?" I replied, "Yes." A few days after this, I was taken very ill, and went to the infirmary. Miss Mary Francis, hearing of my illness, made an errand to come to the infirmary for some thread to mend her apparel, and pretending not to find it, asked me where the Religieuse put it; and desired to know if I had any good news for her. I told her I had not, but as we had permission to assemble for recreation in the afternoon, I would, if I heard any, then inform her. At that instant a Novice opened the door, and Miss Mary Francis excused herself, by pretending that she was looking for the basket of thread. We were not so strictly watched for a few days as we had been, but when Miss Mary Francis exposed her feelings one day before Miss Mary Magdalene and myself, we were again closely watched. I then asked the Superior's permission to write to my friends, and desire them to come and see me, which she granted; and also told me to write whatever I pleased. I prepared a letter accordingly to my sisters, stating that I did not wish to return to the world, but was anxious for a visit from them, &c.

I began now to be much dissatisfied with this Convent. My views of retirement, however, were the same as ever, and I thought I would go to the order of the Sisters of Charity, where Miss Mary Francis was educated, as she had promised to introduce me there. She told me, that should I be called to the public apartments, (as an assistant in ornamental work,) if possible, to slip a billet into Miss I.'s hand, (a scholar from New York,) who would convey it to her; and I must not open my mind to my confessor until I was sure she had left the Community. I asked her if she would take a letter for me into the world; she replied, she dare not, as the Superior would examine her, and not permit any thing to be carried from the Convent into the world We then laid the following plan, to mislead the Superior in regard to our intentions. Miss Mary Francis was to complain to the Superior that I would not give proper attention when at my lessons, and I was to tell her that I could not receive any benefit from Miss Mary Francis, on account of her grief and absence of mind. This we fulfilled to the letter. We also agreed on a signal, by which I should know whether she was going with or without permission. If she went without permission, she was to tie a string around an old book, as if to keep the leaves together, and lay it upon the writing desk; if with permission, she was to make the sign of the cross three times upon her lips. I had intimated my desire to go with her, but she said it would be more prudent for me to endeavor to obtain the Superior's permission to see some of my friends, and I could then consult with them, and arrange matters to suit me. After our conversation, she knelt at the altar of the Blessed Virgin, and begged God to forgive us if we acted wrong in this matter; and said to me, "May we not hope for pardon in this matter, if the Superior can be so wicked as to approach the holy of holies, and yet receive absolution?" She then selected from a book the letters forming her real name, that I might write to her, should I not get an opportunity to give a letter to Miss I. A Religieuse entered and whispered her to come away, and I never saw her afterwards.

When the Bishop next visited the "Community" he said he understood that they were rid of that person who had caused them so much trouble. They all then rejoiced, because Miss Mary Francis had gone. The Bishop asked whither they had sent her. They answered, "To her friends." Nothing more at that time was said about it.

Not long after this, at private confession, I was questioned very particularly in regard to my views of remaining there for life. I told my confessor that I was convinced that order was too austere for me, and immediately burst into tears. He endeavored to comfort me by saying I was not bound to *that* order for life; I could go to *another* order. I asked him if I might see my friends. He answered, "Yes." After receiving a promise from him that I should go to any other order I chose, I consented to take the *vows*. He gave me to understand, that I need take no other vows there than I should at the Con vent of the Sisters of Charity. My reception took place the next day. I refused the white veil, because the Sisters of Charity did not wear it, and it was omitted. The choir was first darkened, and then lighted with wax tapers. The ceremony commenced with chants, prayers, responses, &c. A book was placed in my hands, which contained the vows I was to take. As near as I can recollect, the following is the substance of them:—

"O, almighty and everlasting God, permit me, a worm of the dust, to consecrate myself more strictly to thee this day, in presence of thy most Holy Mother, and Saint Ursula, and all of thy Saints and Martyrs, by living *two years* a *Recluse*, and by instructing young ladies after the manner of Saint Ursula, and by taking upon myself her most holy vows of poverty, chastity, and obedience, which, with thy grace and assistance, I will fulfil."

They all responded, "Amen," and repeated a long office in Latin. I still continued to wear the black garb,* which the Bishop blessed; also a long habit, and a string of rosary beads, which were also blessed by the Bishop. He wished to know, one day, how Miss Mary Agnes did, after taking the *white* vows; to which the Supe rior replied, "Very well." He then con versed about the establishment in Boston, and said that some Sisters of Charity were coming to constitute a Convent either

* The apparel of a Religieuse is always kissed by the wearer, every time of putting on and taking off.

there or at Mount Benedict lower establishment.*

Meanwhile Sister Mary Magdalene was employed in the refectory. According to the Bishop she was a Saint, and he said there was a Saint's body in the tomb, one of the late Sisters', which remained undecayed. I heard the Superior, about this time, tell Miss Mary Magdalene to burn all her treasures,† or she would suffer in purgatory for her self-love; and she was afraid she did not suffer patiently, for she appeared romantic. Mary Magdalene fell prostrate at the Superior's feet, and said she would fulfil any command that should be laid upon her. The Superior gave her a penance to kiss the feet of all the Religieuse, and asked them to say an Ave and a Pater for her; after which

* The Bishop in confession told me I could, if I preferred it, become one of these Sisters.

† The treasures consisted of written prayers, books, papers, a lock of her mother's hair, &c., which she brought from Ireland, and kept in her desk.

she lay prostrate in the refectory until the Angelus rung. One communion morning, as I rose and was dressing, I took some water, as usual, to rinse my mouth, and all at once Mary Magdalene appeared greatly agitated, and even in agony; made signs and crosses to signify that I should commit a sacrilege were I then to approach the communion; and I then recollected that nothing must be taken into the mouth on the morning before this sacrament. I relate this to show the state of her mind. The Superior one day requested the Mother Assistant to get the keys of the tomb, and to have a good place prepared for Mary Magdalene, who forced a smile, saying she should prefer hers near the undecayed Saint's bed.

As time passed on, the Superior became more severe in her treatment, because I objected to pursue my music. My mind had been in such an unhappy state, that I, for a long time, found it impossible to study; and, further, I did not wish to receive instruction, for I had determined not to stay there. I therefore succeeded in obtaining the Superior's permission to occupy my time chiefly with the needle, and assured her that I would again study when I felt better.

On one of the holy days the Bishop came in, and after playing upon his flute, addressed the Superior, styling her Mademoiselle, and wished to know if Mary Magdalene wanted to go to her long home. The Superior beckoned to her to come to them, and she approached on her knees. The Bishop asked her if she felt prepared to die. She replied, "Yes, my Lord; but, with the permission of our Mother, I have one request to make." They told her to say on. She said she wished to be anointed before death, if his Lordship thought her worthy of so great a favor. He said, "Before I grant your request, I have one to make; that is, that you will implore the Almighty to send down from heaven a bushel of *gold*, for the purpose of establishing a college for young men on Bunker Hill. He said he had bought the land for that use, and that all the Sisters who had died had promised to present his request, but had not fulfilled their obligations; "and," says he, "you must shake hands in heaven with all the Sisters who have gone, and be sure and ask them why they have not fulfilled their promise, for I have *waited long enough*; and continue to chant your office with us, while here on earth, which is the sweet communion of Saints." After she had given her pledge and *kissed his feet*, he told the several members of the Community, to think of what they should like best. I was first called to make my request. I had never seen any thing of this kind before, and my feelings were such as I cannot describe, and continuing silent, the Superior *bade* me name it. I then said, I lacked humility, and should wish for that virtue. The Religieuse then made their requests: one asked for grace to fulfil the vow of poverty; another, for obedience; a third, more fervent love for the Mother of God; a fourth, more devotion to her patron Saint; a fifth, more devotion in approaching the altar and host; and so on. The Superior ended it, by making the same request as the Bishop, adding, the purpose intended was, that the gospel of our Lord and Savior might be more extensively propagated, and that all dissenters might be made to turn to the true Church and believe. The conversation then turned upon the Pope, and the Bishop said the Pope would, perhaps, before long, visit this country; and when things were more improved, and his new church finished, he should write to the Pope, &c. He went into a relation of some parts of ecclesiastical history; spoke of the Pope's being the vicegerent of Christ on earth; and that although the wicked one prevailed now, it was designed for good, and the time would come, when all would look to the Pope as their spiritual director on earth. He thought that America rightfully belonged to the Pope, and that his Holiness would take up his residence here at some future day.

Not long after this, Mary Magdalene was anointed for death, and took her vows for life, but she continued to wear, the white veil. I thought it singular that Mary Magdalene should at that time take her *black vows*, (as they called them,) because (as I learned in the Community) she had not been there a *year*; and her wearing the *white veil* after taking them appeared still more singular.

I will endeavor to give some idea of the manner in which she took her vows, and of the anointing. After she had retired to her couch,* the Religieuse walked to the room in procession. Sister St. Clair held a wax taper blazing at her feet, and the Superior knelt at her head with

* I learned that the usual custom was to place them in a black coffin covered with a black pall when they were to take the *black vows*; but in this instance it was omitted.

the vows, which were copied on a half-sheet of paper. The Bishop then came in with both sacraments, all of us prostrating as he passed. After putting the tabernacle upon the little altar which had been placed there for that purpose, he read from a book a great many prayers, all of us responding. He asked her a number of questions about renouncing the world, which she answered. The Superior gave her the vows, and after pronouncing them, she was anointed; Sister Clair laying bare her neck and feet, which the Bishop crossed with holy oil, at the same time repeating Latin. He then gave her the *viaticum*, and ended the ceremony as he commenced, with saying Mass, and passed out, we all prostrating.

She lived rather longer than was expected, but her penances were not remitted. She would frequently kneel and prostrate all night long in the cold infirmary, saying her rosary and other penances, one or two of which I will mention. She wore next her heart a metallic plate, in imitation of a crown of thorns, from which I was given to understand she suffered a sort of martyrdom. This I often saw her kiss and lay on the altar of the crucifix as she retired. Another penance was, the reclining upon a mattress more like a table than a bed. A day or two after this, the Superior, Mother Assistant, and Mary Benedict, ridiculed the appearance of Mary Magdalene, because of the dropsy, which prevented her appearing graceful, and because she was disappointed in not going to heaven sooner. The Superior gave her some linen capes to make, and said, "Do you think you shall stay with us long enough to do these, Sister?" She took them, and said, "Yes, Mamère, I thank you."* Notwithstanding the Superior's severity, she sometimes appeared affectionate. One day I failed in ringing the observances at the usual time. I met

---

* She would often ask permission to take a little water, as she was very thirsty; the Superior always refused it; but still the *obedient* Magdalene replied, "Mamère, I thank you."

the Superior, and fearing she would punish me, I burst into tears. She embraced me very affectionately, and wiped my face with a handkerchief, and said I should not be punished that time. She once told me I might sit at meditation hour, instead of kneeling, as it was very tiresome. She frequently called me *her holy innocent*, because she said I kept the rules of the order, and was persevering in my vocation as a *Recluse.* She said I should see my friend Mrs. G. before long, but I did not see her while I was there.

While in the Convent I asked once or twice for a Bible, but never received any, and never saw one while there. The Bishop often said that the laity were not qualified to expound the Scriptures, and that the *successors* of the apostles *alone* were authorized to interpret them, &c.

The Bishop, in one of his visits, spoke particularly of the cholera. He told us we must watch and pray more fervently, or "the old Scratch would snatch us off with the cholera." It was recreation hour, but Mary Magdalene was at work in the refectory. When she came to the community, she appeared like a person in spasms; she tried to say "Ave Maria," and immediately fainted: we were all very much alarmed. At that moment the bell called us to the choir for visitation and vespers. When I retired, I felt much hurt to see Mary Magdalene in the cold infirmary, but did not dare to express my feelings. Next day, at recreation, the Superior, Mother Assistant, and Mrs. Mary Benedict, made a short visit to Mary Magdalene, and on returning they told us she was better, and in a spiritual sense well; for she had refused taking her portion, or any thing eatable, as she did not wish to nourish her body, because the will of God had been made known to her in a vision We all had the promise of conversing with her, but we were so constantly employed in our various offices that we had no leisure.

The next day, it being my turn to see that all the vessels which contained holy water were filled, &c., I had an opportunity of looking at Mary Magdalene. Her eyes were partly open, and her face very purple; she lay pretty still. I did not dare to speak to her, supposing she would think it a duty to tell of it, as it would be an infraction of the rules. The next night I lay thinking of her, when I was suddenly startled, hearing a rattling noise, as I thought, in her throat. Very soon Sister Martha (the sick Lay Nun) arose, and coming to her, said, "Jesus! Mary! Joseph! receive her soul;" and rang the bell three* times. The spirit of the gentle Magdalene had departed The Superior came, bringing a lighted wax-taper, which she placed in the hand of the deceased. She closed the eyes, and placed

* The bell was struck *three* times to call the Superior, *twice* to call the Mother Assistant, and *once* to call Mrs. Mary Benedict.

a crucifix on the breast. Sister Martha had whispered us to rise, and the Superior, observing my agitation, said, "Be calm, and join with us in prayer; *she* is a happy soul." I knelt accordingly, repeating the litany, until the clock struck two, when we all assembled in the choir, in which was a fire and wax-tapers burning. After meditation, matins, lauds, and prayers, and a Novena (a particular supplication) that our requests might be granted, we assembled for diet, and for the first time we had some toasted bread. We also had recreation granted in the time of silence. The Superior sent for us, and instructed us how to appear at the burial of our Sister Mary Magdalene, and accompanied us to view her corpse. She was laid out in the habit of a professed Nun, in a *black veil;* her hands were tied together, and her vows placed in them. The Superior remarked, that this was done by the Bishop's request. At the evening recreation the Bishop appeared in high spirits, and rejoiced that so happy a soul had at last arrived in heaven; and commenced the "*Dies illæ*," on the piano forte, accompanied by the voices of the others. He told me I should have Miss Mary Magdalene for my intercessor, for she was to be canonized. The Mother Superior permitted me to embrace the Sisters, and gave me the Mother Assistant for my *Mother*. She then presented us with the relics of Saints, that by their means we might gain indulgences. She mentioned a "retreat" as being necessary for our perseverance in a *religious life.*

The second day after this, the coffin was placed in the choir, and the funeral services were performed in the following manner: Dr. O'Flaherty sang the office, while the Bishop chanted it. Father Taylor officiated at the altar. Four or five of the altar boys were present, and dressed in altar robes, &c.; two of them held wax tapers, a third holy water, a fourth a crucifix. One swung incense in the censer over the corpse, and another, at the same time, sprinkled holy water upon it. We performed our part by saying the "Dies illæ." The coffin* was then carried to the tomb by two Irishmen. The Bishop, Priests, and others followed, singing, and carrying lighted tapers and a large crucifix. The corpse was also followed by some of the young ladies from the public schools, while the Religieuse remained in the Convent. After depositing the coffin in the tomb, the clergy retired to dinner. We were permitted, at recreation, to hear the clergy converse on various subjects. The Superior told us that the customary libera and prayers for faithful souls departed might be omitted, as the Bishop said Magdalene's soul had gone immediately to heaven. The Novices were permitted to relate visions of guardian angels, &c. At the next evening

* My feelings were much hurt to witness the manner in which the lid of the coffin was *forced* down to its place. The corpse had swollen much, and become too large for the coffin.

recreation the Bishop again visited us, and appeared in very good spirits, played on his flute and sung. He soon went away, and the Superior said he only came to cheer up our spirits.

Having only a few minutes to stay at confession, I had until this time kept the secret of my friend Mary Francis; but the Bishop perceiving that I grew more discontented, endeavored to comfort me, by saying that I was not *bound* to *that* order; but he wished to know more particularly my reasons for disliking it, and began to threaten me with judgments; and observing my agitation, said he *must* know what lay so heavily on my mind. He asked me if it was any thing connected with the sickness and death of Mary Magdalene. I told him "No, not that in particular; I do not like the Superior." He said I must tell him instantly all the wicked thoughts that had disturbed my mind, and asked me various improper questions, the meaning of which

I did not *then* understand, and which I decline mentioning. I was so confused that I inadvertently spoke Mary Francis' name, and begged his pardon for listening to her; and he immediately exclaimed, "Ah! I know all; confess to me what she told you, and do not dare to deceive me; you cannot deceive God." I told him *nearly* all that had passed between Mary Francis and myself. He said that Mary Francis was not a fit subject for any order, and they were obliged to send her away; that she was deranged, and I had done very wrong in listening to an insane person. He said I could not go to the order she mentioned, and that I would be more happy with the Sisters of Charity who were coming to reside here. He said that worldlings hated me for the good part I had chosen, and would ridicule me should I go back to the world, and then repeated some scripture texts. I still persisted in saying it was my determination not to remain in that order, and I told him

I disliked the Superior; and he gave me a penance to perform. I was desirous at that time to have them think me obedient, or I should not have condescended to such humiliations. My motive was *prudence*, not want of courage, for by this time I had become disgusted with the life I led, and their manner of proceeding.

The next time the Bishop was with us, he requested me to sing any favorite tune I chose. I sang the "Ode on Science," which, every one knows, is highly patriotic. At the close of the first stanza, he spoke a few words in French to the Superior, who made a signal for me to stop; but not understanding her, I continued, until she had made several signals, when I perceived she was evidently displeased with my singing, and then recalled the words which I supposed were offensive.

One day the Superior asked me what it was that lay so heavily on my mind, as the Mother Assistant had previously found me in tears while at our examination of conscience. I excused myself by replying I was thinking of my dear mother, (which, though true, was not the cause of my grief.) She then left me, but not without distrust, the eyes of the Community being upon me. The next time we met at recreation, one of them remarked she hoped there was not another *Judas* among them. I endeavored to betray no emotion, but they still mistrusted I had other views; for while sitting at my diet in the refectory, I observed my food was of a kind that I had never seen before. It consisted of several balls of a darkish color, about the size of a nutmeg, of a bitter astringent taste; what they were I never knew I ate them as I did my other diet, and strove to exhibit no fearful sensations.

A few days after the death of Mary Magdalene, her desk was brought forward, that the Superior might examine it, and distribute its contents to those she considered the most worthy. She gave to each one some little relic, and to Miss Mary Joseph, sister to Magdalene, some letters which she had composed to be read, as the Superior said, after her death. They were quite affecting, and caused Mary Joseph to weep much, for which the Superior reprimanded her.

Some days after this, the Superior sent for me to practise music, and then made a signal for me to follow her into the Bishop's room. This room is separated from the others by shutters, with curtains drawing on the chapel side. When I had kissed her feet, she desired to know why I cried at my practice in the choir. I rather imprudently answered, "I could not tell; I did not cry much." (It then struck me, she could not have seen me, as I was *alone.*) I said I was very cold,* particularly my feet; and I had been praetising "Blue-eyed Mary," and was af-

* The rooms were seldom comfortably warmed, and at times I suffered much from the cold.

fected by the words. She said that what I asserted was false, and commanded me to tell her the true cause, *in a moment;* and pulling the handkerchief from my hand, she bade me kneel and tell her at once, or I should be punished. I was so frightened by the threats and manner of the Superior, that I sobbed aloud, and blood gushed from my nose and mouth. She then seized and shook me by the arm, and seated me, saying, "Hush! be calm, or the young ladies may hear you as they pass the door to go to their practice." She asked me again and again to tell her why I shed tears in the choir, and why I felt such a repugnance to communicate my thoughts. I replied, because I had made a *promise* not to tell, and I could not break it. The Superior turned pale, but suppressing her feelings, bade me break that promise directly, and asked to whom I had made it. I replied I could not tell any one but my confessor. Says she, embracing me, "What! my *dear* Sister, not obey your Superior! tell me, my *dear*, and I will stand *responsible* for you before the judgment seat. To whom did you make the promise?—to Mary Magdalene or Mary Francis?" She also asked me if I had related all the causes of my discontent in confession. I replied, "Not all," and began to weep again. She endeavored to console me, saying she could not heal my wounds unless I opened my whole feelings to her; and comparing her words to those of our divine Redeemer, took me by the hand, and with seeming affection told me to unfold all my feelings to her, as to an own mother; and said she should think it her duty to stay by me until I should relate the cause of my grief, that she might pour into my heart a heavenly balm, &c. I told her I had not seen or heard from my friends, to whom I had written. She said that was nothing to the point; she was my friend; and asked me if I called persons who insulted the house of God my friends. I replied, "No." She then said one person had been there who called herself my sister, and who threw pebbles at the Convent. She also mentioned another person, who came with my sister, and whom she said she would not take to "*wipe her feet on.*"* After

---

* I learn from my sister that while I was in the Convent she and another young lady went there to invite me to my sister M.'s wedding. She asked the portress if I could be seen at that hour, who replied she would see, and asked her to walk in, inquired her name, &c., went out, and soon returned with the answer that the scholars were not permitted to come to the parlor that day. My sister told her it was important that she should see me, and she could not come away without. The portress left the room, returned, closed the shutters, retired, and presently the Superior entered, walking between two servants, and made signs for my sister to approach, inquiring hers and the other lady's names, and their business. On being informed, she mentioned that I could not be seen, but she would deliver any message my sister desired; that the young ladies never violated the rules for the sake of seeing company, and that I did not wish to see any worldly friends, or have any communication with them; that my mind was wholly occupied with heavenly things; that I was perfectly happy, and "*growing as fat as butter;*" that I was fast improving in my studies, learning music, and drawing, (untrue.) In consequence of my sister's weeping, and desiring her to name a time when I could be seen, the Superior said she would go and inquire whether I desired to see her. The Superior soon returned, and told my sister that I did not wish to see her, or any worldly relative; but the Superior told her that if I chose I could come to

making this observation, she left me for a few moments, to compose myself. Returning, she asked if I knew where I was, and if I had concluded to obey her, or break my vow of obedience and be *severely* punished. I answered, "No! Mamère, I will tell all I can remember;" for I judged from her threats and looks that I should be confined in a cellar, or have something more severe than usual inflicted upon me. The rules of the order also led me to think so. But notwithstanding my fear of the Superior, I still kept secret the real name of Miss Mary Francis, and her promise of writing to Mrs. G. or my friends respecting my situation. She then dismissed me for a while. But my thoughts soon whispered

---

the wedding. They both left the Convent with the impression that I was a public scholar, and could leave when I chose; and thought it passing strange that I should refuse to see them, as I had, before going to the Convent, requested them to visit me. My sister imagined that I had become so infatuated with the Catholic religion as to lose all sisterly affection for those who were averse to it, and went away weeping.

me that our "*Ghostly Father*" (as our Directory taught us to call him) had made the Superior acquainted with what passed in secret confession, because without such knowledge she never could have used such threatening language, and never could have been displeased, as she was, at words which I had used in secret confession *alone* with the Bishop. She asked me how I dared to converse with Mary Francis on the slate. Now she never could have known this only from the Bishop. I was never fully aware of their arts in getting at secrets by confession until they became too visible to be misunderstood. I then became more reserved, and the Superior remarked that I did not show so much frankness of manner as formerly; the reason of which the reader will understand to be, that every eye was on me. A different course I could not adopt, having lost *confidence* in my confessor. I did not follow his advice, but resolved to follow, as nearly as

I could conscientiously, the advice of Mary Francis, being confident she was my friend.

I felt a repugnance at the idea of re turning to the world, supposing tha many would believe me a person romar tic and visionary, and inexperienced the ways of the world, and therefore un for society. And I was also particular averse to taking this step, because the solemn promise of seclusion which had taken. Nevertheless, I resolved t leave that Convent, and write to Miss Mary Francis from my friend Mrs. G.'s, but was undetermined whether I should return to the world. I had reason to think that my letters were never sent to my friends, and determined to convey one privately. I stole a few moments and hastily wrote some lines with my pencil, and hid them behind the altar; but the billet was discovered, and I never heard from it.

It was my turn that week to read a

"lecturess." A book was placed before me in the refectory, called "Rules of Saint Augustine," and the place marked to read was concerning a Religieuse receiving letters clandestinely. I could not control my feelings, for what I read was very affecting. At this time we were directed to remain in the refectory, instead of assembling in the community, and told to repeat "Hail Mary" before a picture. The Superior and Mother Assistant consented to have me practise music no more during the cold weather. They also permitted me to wear warmer clothing.

One day as I was sitting alone in the refectory, in the time of silence, the Superior came in, and after kneeling and extending her arms in the form of a cross, she kissed the floor, and rising, walked towards the door; returning, she seated herself on the bench beside me. I asked her if I should bring a chair; she answered, "No," and inquired how I felt, and why I changed color while at the table. I replied that my mouth was very sore, and it hurt me to read. She wished to know what made my mouth sore. I told her I thought it was something I had eaten. She said, *laughingly*, it was the canker, and asked if it was not sent as a judgment for some sin. I replied that I did not know; I had not felt very well for some days, and thought it was partly owing to want of exercise. She then sent Sister Martha to conduct me into a room at the farther part of the Convent, for the first time, called a "*mangle room.*" There were some Sisters there kneeling in devotion, and one turning a machine used for pressing clothes, instead of ironing them, called a *mangle.* She presented me with some altar laces, and told me to have them prepared for the altar the next day at the ringing of the bell. While there I was watched very narrowly; but as I had gathered from the Superior's conversation, at different times, that the gates were watched by the porters and dogs, which were of great value to the Convent, I did not dare, then, to make my escape, but appeared as cheerful as possible. The Sisters appeared very happy, it being a day of recreation in the Community, and the celebration of some great Saint. The Superior, as she passed her portrait, remarked, that she never looked at it but that it reminded her of smiling. She appeared in unusually good spirits, and gave us permission to wish each other happy feasts, not of luxury and feasting, in the common acceptation of the terms, but of prayers to the Saints to free us from purgatory. In the course of the Superior's conversation, she said she had read in the newspapers of a new law which had been passed, that no person who was under the age of twenty-eight or thirty years should be allowed to keep any school The Mother Assistant approved of this law, and said it was good as it would remove the difficulty which overseers had with young teachers who were unfit to take charge of a school, particularly the discipline.

I would here confess my fault (if a fault it was) of not acknowledging all my obligations in secret confession, and of *pretending* to think Mary Francis deranged; and also of acquiescing in the Superior's commands in her presence with feigned humility. I did this that my design should not be suspected.

A letter was read to the Community, that was addressed to the Superior, from Bishop P., of Emmetsburg. In it he rejoiced to learn that the "Community" was set free of *that person* who was deranged, and whose disposition he had known to his sorrow from her youth. He lamented the departure of Magdalene, who no doubt was a Saint reigning in glory, after what she had been willing to suffer to gain salvation.* I was sent for

* Since leaving the Convent I have written to Miss Mary Francis for information in regard to this letter, but have received no satisfactory answer. I have however received from her three letters.

to attend the Superior in the Bishop's room. after Mass. She was folding his cassoe and robe. When I entered, she bade me do as my Directory taught, and said I had let *trifles* make an impression upon me, and weak minds only allowed trifles to affect them. Giving me the let ter, she bade me tell her what I thought of it. I read it, and said I could not be lieve what Mary Francis had told me, if she were deranged, but yet I had rather go to the Convent where she was edu cated than stay at that on Mount Benedict. She asked me if I thought of going without protection? I begged of her to let me see some of my friends *there*, or permit me to return to the world. After saying she had sent my letters* to my friends, who, if they wished, could come there and see me, she told me not to trouble myself, for the Bishop would soon be there, and I could talk with him about it.†

---

* My friends never received any letter from me.

† I cannot remember all that passed in confession, for I was at

One Sabbath after Mass, while we were in the choir repeating the examination of conscience or monthly review, I was called in a whisper into the community, with the rest of the Sisters, but pretended not to hear. The others went in while I remained. I heard the Bishop speak to them as they went in. But I had absented myself from confession and communion that day, and did not wish to see the Bishop on account of his previous language. After the doors had been opened several times, one of the Religieuse (Sister Martha*) came in and knelt with me. The bell then rang, and I went into the refectory, waiting as usual

---

this time much confused; however, the Bishop asked me how I should like to go to a Convent in Canada, which I objected to.

* I will not presume to say much about Sister Martha, as I never conversed with her, and therefore was not so able to judge of her sufferings, &c. She was a professed Lay Religieuse, and I believe an American. She was called the Portress, and one of those (I learned) who chose rather to be a doorkeeper than to dwell among the wicked. She, together with three of the Choir Religieuse, lodged in the infirmary with me. While she slept there, she (as did Magdalene) coughed at intervals during the night. Sister Martha often approached the Superior kneeling and weeping.

for the Mother Assistant's instructions in the Latin offiee. Sister Martha soon entered, and asked if I knew where the Mother Assistant was, and whether I had been into the community since Mass. I replied, No, but was waiting for the Mother Assistant. After saying office I went down to the refectory to string some rosary beads, and afterwards returned to the choir, where the Novices were telling their beads. The Superior came in to join in devotion, and remained until diet As we were proceeding to diet, I accidentally *touched* the Superior; she looked at me, and appeared much displeased. At recreation the Religieuse were very desirous to learn the state of my mind. I strove to appear unembarrassed, and answered their questions with seeming ignorance. I was not censured for my transgression of the rules, nor was any remark made upon it.

In the evening we were permitted to sit in the community, which had been warmed. After repeating the offices, and during the time of silence, a dog barked in front of the community, and we heard a noise like some one thumping upon the doors. The Religieuse fell down before the altar, and appeared much frightened. I kept my seat, but at that moment heard the window raised, and the Superior ask who was there. No answer was made to her inquiry. I then felt somewhat alarmed, but endeavored to betray as little fear as possible. What this noise was, or for what reason it was made, I never could learn, but I have supposed it was done to see if I was easily alarmed. The like had several times occurred.

About this time the martyrologies of some Saints were read at table; also the history of Saints who had been tempted by Satan. Perhaps it may be well to relate one or two. A certain Saint, who was strongly tempted by Satan, retired to a desert, and confined himself to a cell, scarcely large enough for him to lie at ease. He retired here for pious purposes. After mortifying his body for a long time, he prayed for rain that he might quench his thirst, which was granted. A bird came and brought him food, which renewed his strength, and he returned to his Monastery, and was never more troubled with the temptations of Satan.

Some noblemen once invited a poor wandering monk, who was begging for the Monastery, to dine with them on Friday. They helped him to meat; he made the sign of the cross, refusing to eat it. They asked the reason, and drawing their swords, threatened his life unless he did eat it. He told them if they would allow him a few minutes that he might pray, and give him a pewter plate to cover the meat, he would eat it. After praying a few minutes that the meat might become fish, he took off the plate, and behold it was fish; and he then sat down and ate, and they believed him an inspired man.

Many accounts of those who had become Saints were so disagreeable and even revolting, that I will not attempt to relate or describe them.

As several of my friends desire to learn something concerning the scholars, I will relate what little I know. I never had permission to enter any of the rooms in the recluse apartments, except those before named, and never to the public apartments, except on examination days, when the Superior and Bishop were present. During one vacation, the young ladies who remained were permitted to visit the Community, to give the members presents.* I never spoke to them but to thank them for a present. They were sometimes at vacation permitted to enter the Community and embrace the Religieuse.

Complaints were often brought to the Superior while at recreation, and sometimes repeated aloud. They were generally violations of the *rules*, which were very strict. They were sometimes pun-

* Although we received presents, we were not allowed to keep them.

ished for refusing to say prayers to the Saints, which they said their parents disapproved of; also for refusing to read Roman Catholic history. A Miss T., of C., was brought to the Superior, and reprimanded for writing her discontents to her friends. The Superior destroyed one half the letter, and gave me the blank leaf to write a prayer on. Another was reprimanded severely because she had said to the other young misses she should be glad when the time came for her to leave the Convent, &c. The Superior, shaking her severely, obliged her to kneel and perform an act of contrition, by kissing the floor, and saying that she was very sorry that she had offended her teachers, and begged the forgiveness of all.

Some of the young ladies were apparently great favorites of the Superior and Bishop. They sometimes sent for them to bestow presents and caress them. One young lady, of whom the Bishop was guardian, was treated very ill. I often saw her in tears, and once heard the teacher tell the Superior that it was because she had no dress suitable to wear into the world to see her friends. She was designed, as I learned, to be a teacher in a Convent in Canada.

A number of the young ladies were unhappy, whose names I have forgotten. I learned that they disliked the discipline.

After this the Superior was sick of the influenza, and I did not see her for two or three days. I attended to my offices as usual, such as preparing the wine and the water, the chalice, host, holy water, and vestments, &c. One day, however, I had forgotten to attend to this duty at the appointed hour, but recollecting it, and fearing lest I should offend the Superior by reason of negligence, I asked per mission to leave the room, telling a Novice that our Mother had given me per mission to attend to it; she answered, "O yes, Sister, you can go then." I went immediately to the chapel, and was arranging the things for Mass, which was to take place the next day. While busily employed, I heard the adjoining door open, and the Bishop's voice distinctly. Being conscious that I was there at the wrong hour, I kept as still as possible, lest I should be discovered. While in this room I overheard the following conversation between the Bishop and Superior. The Bishop, after taking snuff in his usual manner, began by saying, "Well, well, what does Agnes say? how does she appear?" I heard *distinctly* from the Superior in reply, that, "According to all appearances, she is either possessed of *insensibility* or great *command.*" The Bishop walked about the room, seeming much displeased with the Superior, and cast many severe and improper reflections upon Mary Francis, who, it was known, had influenced me; all which his Lordship will well remember. He then told the Superior that the esta-

'blishment was in its infancy; and that it would not do to have such reports go abroad as these persons would carry; that Agnes must be taken care of; that they had better send her to Canada, and that a carriage could cross the line in two or three days. He added, by way of repetition, that it would not do for the Protestants to get hold of those things and make another "fuss." He then gave the Superior instructions how to entice me into the carriage, and they soon both left the room and I heard no more.

The reader may well judge of my feelings at this moment; a young and inexperienced female, shut out from the world, and entirely beyond the reach of friends; threatened with speedy transportation to another country, and involuntary confinement for life, with no power to resist the immediate fulfilment of the startling conspiracy I had overheard. It was with much difficulty that I controlled my feelings, but aware of the importance of not betraying any knowledge of what had taken place, I succeeded in returning to the refectory unsuspected. I now became firmly impressed that unless I could contrive to break away from the Convent soon, it would be forever too late; and that every day I remained rendered my escape more difficult.

The next day I went to auricular confession, not without trembling and fear, lest I should betray myself. But having committed my case to God, I went somewhat relieved in my feelings. At a previous confession I had refused to go to Canada, but at this time, in reply to the Bishop's inquiry, I answered that I would consider the subject · for I thought it wrong to evince any want of fortitude, especially when I had so much need of it. I did not alter my course of conduct, fearing that if I appeared perfectly contented I should be suspected of an intention to escape.

It was my turn during that week to

officiate in the offices. While reading, I felt something rise in my throat, which two or three times I tried to swallow, but it still remained. I felt alarmed, it being what I had never before experienced.* At recreation I was asked what ailed me, and replied that I could not tell; but I de scribed my feelings, and was told I was vaporish.

They were very desirous that week to know if my feelings were changed. I said they were, and endeavored to make it appear to them that Satan had left me. But in reality I feared I should never escape from them, though I had determined to do so the first opportunity.

I was in the habit of talking in my sleep, and had often awoke and found the Religieuse kneeling around my couch, and was told that they were praying for me Fearing lest I should let fall some word or words which would betray me, I tied a handkerchief around my face, de-

* I have since named the circumstance to a physician, who says it was *fear* alone.

termining if observed to give the appearance of having the teeth ache, and so avoid detection. For some days I was not well, and my mind, as may naturally be supposed, sympathized with my body, and many things occurred that were to me unpleasant, which I shall pass unnoticed.

But what I have now to relate is of importance. A few days after, while at my needle in the refectory, I heard a carriage drive to the door of the Convent, and heard a person step into the Superior's room. Immediately the Superior passed lightly along the passage which led to the back entry, where the men servants or porters were employed, and reprimanded them in a loud tone for something they were doing. She then opened the door of the refectory, and seemed indifferent about entering, but at length seated herself be side me, and began conversation, by saying, "Well, my dear girl, what do you think of going to see your friends?" I said, "What friends, Mamère?" said she, "You would like to see your friends Mrs. G., and Father B., and talk with them respecting your call to another order." Before I had time to answer, she commenced taking off my garb, telling me she was in haste, and that a carriage was in waiting to convey me to my friends. I answered, with as cheerful a countenance as I could assume, "O, Mamère, I am sorry to give you so much trouble; I had rather see them here first." While we were conversing I heard a little bell ring several times The Superior said, "Well, my dear, make up your mind; the bell calls me to the parlor." She soon returned, and asked if I had made up my mind to go. I answered, "No, Mamère." She then said I had failed in obedience to her, and as I had so often talked of going to another order with such a person as Mary Francis, I had better go immediately; and again she said, raising her voice, "You have failed in respect to your

Superior; you must recollect that I am a lady of *quality*, brought up in opulence, and accustomed to all the luxuries of life." I told her that I was very sorry to have listened to any thing wrong against her dignity. She commanded me to kneel, which I did; and if ever tears were a relief to me they were then. She stamped upon the floor violently, and asked, if I was innocent, why I did not go to communion. I told her I felt unworthy to go to communion at that time.* The bell again rang, and she left the room, and in a few moments returning, desired me to tell her immediately what I thought of doing, for as she had promised to protect me forever, she must know mv mind. She then mentioned that the carriage was still in waiting. I still declined going, for I was convinced

---

* My eyes were opened; I found myself in an error, and had been too enthusiastic in my first views of a Convent life. I was discontented with my situation, and was using some deception towards the Superior and the Religieuse, in order to effect an escape; therefore I did not feel worthy to attend communion.

their object was not to carry me to Mrs. G. and Priest B., to consult about another order, but directly to Canada. I told her I had concluded to ask my confessor's advice, and meditate on it some longer. She rather emphatically said, "You can meditate on it if you please, and do as you like about going to see your friends." She said that my sister had been there and did not wish to see me. Our conversation was here interrupted by the entrance of a Novice. The Superior then gave me my choice, either to remain on Mount Benedict, or go to some other order, and by the next week to make up my mind, as it remained with me to decide. She then gave me a heavy penance to perform, which was, instead of going to the choir as usual at the ringing of the bell, to go to the mangle room and repeat "Ava Marias" while turning the mangle. While performing my penance, Sister Martha left the room, and soon returning, said she had orders to release me from my penance, and to direct me to finish my meditations on the picture of a Saint, which she gave me. But instead of saying the prayers that I was bidden, I fervently prayed to be delivered from their wicked hands.

They appeared much pleased with my supposed reformation, and I think they believed me sincere The Superior, as a test of my humility, kept me reading; that is, made no signal for me to stop, until the diet was over, when a plate of apple parings, the remnant of her dessert, was brought from the Superior's table, and the signal given for me to lay down my book and eat them.* I ate a *few* of them *only*, hoping they might think my abstaining from the remainder self-denial in me, and not suspect me of discontent or disobedience. I performed all my penances with apparent cheerfulness.

The Bishop visited the Convent on the

---

* This was the second time I had been presented with apple parings by the Superior.

next holy day, and on their remarking that he had been absent some time, he made many excuses; one of which was, he had been engaged in collecting money to establish the order of the "Sisters of Charity" where the "Community" once lived; and he spoke of the happiness of the life of a "Religieuse" of this order. After he played on the piano, "Away with Melancholy," the Superior asked me to play, and the Bishop said, "By all means." I complied, but my voice faltered through fear, when Miss Mary Benedict apologized for me, by saying I had not practised much lately, on account of the Mother Assistant's engagements, and the young ladies occupying all the instruments. She showed the Bishop a robe which I had been busy in working for him. He said I must not on any account neglect my music. After telling one of his stories about a monk who had disobeyed the rules of his order until Satan took possession of him he left us, saying he hoped "old Scratch" would not take possession of our hearts as he did that monk's, and hoped that we should never have another Judas in the Community.

Some days after the conversation which I heard between the Bishop and Superior while behind the altar, I was in the refectory at my work, and heard the noise of the porters, who were employed sawing wood, and I conjectured the gate might be open for them. I thought it a good opportunity to escape, which I contemplated doing in this manner, viz.: to ask permission to leave the room, and as I passed the entry, to secrete about my habit a hood which hung there, that would help to conceal part of my garb from particular observation; then to feign an errand to the infirmarian from the Superior, as I imagined I could escape by the door of the infirmary. This plan formed, and just as I was going, I heard a band of music, playing, as it seemed, in front of the Convent. I heard the young ladies assembling in the parlor, and the porters left their work, as I supposed, for the noise of the saws ceased. I felt quite revived, and was more confident I should be able to escape without detection, even should it be necessary to get over the fence. I feigned an errand, and asked permission of Miss Mary Austin to leave the room,* which she granted. I succeeded in secreting the hood, and the book in which Miss Mary Francis had left her address, and then knocked at the door three times which led to the lay apartments. A person came to the door, who appeared in great distress.†

---

* Sister Mârtha (the sick Religieuse) was scouring the floor at this time, which I saw was quite too hard for her. Not long after I left, I inquired after her, and learned she was no more.

† This was Sarah S , (a domestic) who appeared very unhappy while I was in the Convent. I often saw her in tears, and learned from the Superior that she was *sighing* for the *veil*. When I saw my brother I informed him of this circumstance, and he soon found who she was, and ascertained that some ladies in Cambridge had been to see the Superior, who used to them pretty much the same language she did to my sister I have since seen her. She is still under the influence of the Roman Church, but assures me that she did not refuse to see the ladies, as the Superior had represented to them, and she wept because of ill health, &c.

I asked her where Sister Bennet and Sister Bernard were; she left me to find them. I gave the infirmarian to understand that the Superior wished to see her, and I desired her to go immediately to her room. These gone. I unlocked and passed out the back door, and as the gate appeared shut, I climbed upon the *slats* which confined the grape vines to the fence; but they gave way, and falling to the ground, I sprained my wrist. I then thought I would try the gate, which I found unfastened, and as there was no one near it, I ran through, and hurried to the nearest house. In getting over the fences between the Convent and this house, I fell and hurt myself badly. On reaching the house, I fell exhausted upon the door step; but rising as soon as possible, I opened the door, and was allowed to enter. I inquired if Catholics lived there; one answered, "No." For some time I could answer none of their questions, being so much exhausted.

As soon as they understood that I requested protection, they afforded me every assistance in their power. I had been only a few moments there, when I heard the alarm bell ringing at the Convent. On looking out at the window, we saw two of the porters searching in the canal with long poles. After searching some time they returned to the Convent, and I saw their dogs scenting my course.

While at that house I looked in a glass, and was surprised, nay, frightened, at my own figure, it was so *pale* and *emaciated.**

Notwithstanding my wrist being sprained, I wrote a few lines to Mrs. G., whom I still supposed my friend, begging her to come to my relief, for I did not wish my father and sisters to see me in my present condition. I thanked God that he had inclined his ear unto me, and delivered me out of the hands of the wicked. But

* It will be perceived that this does not correspond with what the Superior told my sister.

here was not an end of my afflictions. Mrs. G. came in the evening to convey me to her house. She would not allow me to say any thing about my escape at Mr. K.'s, and wished me to return to the Convent that night. I resolved not to go. After whispering a long time to me about the importance of secrecy, she left Mr. K.'s, as we supposed, for home; but she soon returned, saying she at first intended to leave me at Mr. K.'s, but had concluded to take me home with her, as she desired some further conversation. Her manners appeared very strange, yet I did not distrust her friendship. Before leaving Mr. K.'s, she requested me to obtain from them a promise not to say any thing about my escape, which I did.

After I arrived at Mrs. G.'s, I showed her my wounds, and my feet, which had been frozen, and told her I did not find the Convent what I had expected. She seemed to sympathize with me, and to do all in her power for my recovery. She did not then urge me to say much as I was quite weak.

The next morning, the Convent boy on horseback came galloping up to the house, and delivered to Mrs. G. a letter from the Superior, and was very particular, as he said he had orders not to give it to any one except to her. She refused to tell me its contents, and sent directly for a chaise, to go to the Convent. She took with her the religious garb I had worn on my head, and the book containing Miss Mary Francis' name * Meanwhile I endeavored to compose myself, and wrote to Miss Mary Francis, agreeably to my promise, informing her of my afflictions, and of my reluctance to return to the bustle of the world. I proposed to her some questions, and requested her advice. I wrote that I could not think otherwise than that the

* This book I brought away because Mary Francis had pricked hers and her father's *real* name out in it, and I wished to refer to it, in order to write her. I took it from my writing desk, and slipped it into my pocket.

Superior and Bishop were very wicked. I did not write much, thinking her confessor might advise her not to answer it, as it was probable that the Superior would write to him; and I was anxious to convince Mrs. G. that Mary Francis thought as I did, for Mrs. G. would not permit me to say one word against the Superior or Bishop; and I was resolved to ascertain if Mary Francis was living and happy. When Mrs. G. returned from the Convent she said the Superior had too exalted an opinion of me to think I would say any thing against the institution, and she had sent me a *present*, as she still considered me one of her flock; and if I had gone astray, she should do every thing she could for me, in a temporal as well as in a spiritual sense, if I would repent. My words were just these: "I cannot receive any present from the Superior; she is a wicked woman, and I do not believe her friendship pure." At this moment Priest B. drove to the door, and desired to see me. I did not think myself in danger, and conversed with him; but I soon found that he had seen the Superior and Bishop. He said that as he was my sponsor he considered it his duty to advise me, and hoped I was not going to break my *vows* to God and *expose* myself to the world; because, if I did, I should be ridiculed and laughed at. He said he had before conveyed a Novice to the "Sisters of Charity," and would convey me to them, or to some other retired place which I might choose, and that he was deeply concerned for my welfare. I told him I could not think of going anywhere then, as my health would not allow any exposure to the cold, and that Mrs. G. thought it best I should remain with her until I was better, when I should visit my father. He then exclaimed, "What letter is this?" taking up and reading the one I had written to Mary Francis. After reading it, he appeared surprised, and desired to know how I came in possession of her name He said he should have seen me at the Con vent had he known I was discontented;

and that if the Superior had done wrong, it was no reason I should do so, by speaking against the Convent or those connected with it. He then shook hands with me, and said he would converse with me again when I was more composed, and left the house.

I soon began to suspect by Mrs. G.'s manners that she was not my friend, and that if she had an opportunity she would deliver me into the hands of the Catholics; for I learned from her little daughter that her mother had given her to the Catholic Church, because the Superior had offered to educate her, free of expense; and that her mother was acquainted with the Superior before I went to the Convent. Now this I did not know before, and I began to be more guarded, and to fear that all belonging to the Romish Church were alike. When I gave Mrs. G. the letter to send to the post-office, she asked if I was afraid she would break it open; and at another time afterwards, she told me I was afraid she would poison me, because I refused to take medicine, which I thought I did not need. Such thoughts did not occur to my mind.

In a day or two Priest B. again came, and after much persuasion from Mrs. G. I consented to see him. At first he appeared very pleasant, said he had come to render me assistance, and begged, as I valued my religion and reputation, to take his advice. I told him that I wished none of his assistance or advice; that I should go to my brother's, at East Cambridge, as soon as possible; that as it respected my religion, I did not believe in one which justified its followers in doing wrong; and that I was not at all concerned that my reputation would be injured on that account by returning to the world. He affected considerable contempt for my aged parent, and ridiculed many things which he said he had heard of my father. And he said,* "Is it possible that a young lady wishes to have her name made pub-

* He informed me I should be anathematized publicly if I did not repent.

lic?" I answered, "You very well know I should shrink from such a thing, but I should rather return to the world and ex pose myself to its scorn, than remain sub ject to the commands of a tyrant." "Then," said he, "if you are determined to return to the world, you may go to ruin there for all I can do; and rely upon it. you will shed tears of blood in consequence of the step you have taken, if you do not repent and confess all at the secret tribunal of God." I told him I should confess to none but God, and that my conscience prompted me to do as I had done. He asked me if I would go with him to the Superior, as she wanted to see me. I replied, "No, I will not, for I believe you or any other Catholic would (if directed) take my life, were it in your power, as truly as I believe I am living, and I will not trust myself in your clutches again." At these words he turned pale, and asked me what I had seen or heard at the Convent that made me think so. I refused to say more, and retired at his exclamation that it would be *death* to me. Mrs. G. endeavored to console me with the assurance that he meant right, and that it would, they feared, be death to my soul.

Mrs. G. afterwards accused me of endeavoring, at the time of my escape, to induce Sister Bernard to leave the Convent. The Superior sent me some articles of wearing apparel, which for a time I was obliged to accept. My sister called; she had been at the Convent, and was informed that I was at Mrs. G.'s. She was overjoyed to see me, but much grieved because (as she thought) I had refused to see her at the Convent. I endeavored to calm her, and promised to explain all another time, assuring her my affection was not diminished, and that I should soon visit her. I did not then explain to her the manner of my leaving the Convent. It being late in the evening, she soon returned home. The Misses K. also called, and by their conversation I feared they would inform my father of my situation, before I should be well and prepared to see him; and I did not wish to grieve him with a knowledge of what had taken place. Mrs. G. said she expected my father would rave at her for having advised me as she had done, if he should find me at her house.

A Catholic lady, who had stood my sponsor, and who brought a letter from Mary Francis,* called, and conveyed me to her house in Charlestown, where my father and brother soon found me, and desired I would return to my friends, which I did in the evening. Before leaving, however, I called on Priest B., and told him that I could never think of again attending the Romish Church, giving my reasons, and adding that I had been deceived in their religion, and in those who believed it; that I wished to take my leave of him, with the hope that he would not think I indulged any wrong feelings towards them, or that I desired to

* This letter had been broken open.

injure the Romish Church, but sincerely hoped they would reform. I told him this while he sat in the confessional. He remained unmoved, and would not allow that I had been treated ill. He said that I could not but know that the step I had taken would be a great injury to the Convent. I assured him that it was not to be charged to me, but to the Superior and Bishop, who by their conduct had compelled me to take that step. I also told him that I believed it had been his intention to deliver me again into their hands, but I had broken the chains which bound me, and felt free; and that I should always be thankful that I had delivered myself from the bondage of what I should consider to be a *Romish yoke*, rather than the true cross of Christ.

After I had returned to my brother's, Mrs. G. sent to me by her little daughter some money, which she said I had given to the Superior. Five dollars of this sum and some wearing apparel I considered as not my own, and sent them back with a note to Madam St. George, stating that I declined receiving any thing from them as *presents*, but if they would return what wearing apparel, &c. *belonged* to me, it would be properly acknowledged.

And now I have endeavored, to the extent of my ability, to give a true and faithful account of what fell under my observation during my sojourn among the Catholics, and especially during my residence at the Monastery on Mount Benedict. And I leave it with the reader to judge of my motives for becoming a member of the Ursuline Community, and for renouncing it.

If, in consequence of my having for a time strayed from the *true religion*, I am enabled to become an humble instrument in the hands of God in warning others of the errors of Romanism, and preventing even *one* from falling into its *snares*, and from being *shrouded* in its delusions, I shall feel richly rewarded.

LETTER TO IRISH CATHOLICS.

[CONDENSED FROM A BOSTON PAPER.]

I AM told that it will be of no use to write letters to you, because so many of you cannot read. But there are also many of you who *can* read. I write to *them;* and I hope they will read my letters to the rest.

But why have you not been taught to read? You and your forefathers have had Roman Catholic Priests for a thousand years What have they been doing? Why have they not taught you, or taken care to have you taught by others? What have they done with all the money which you and your fathers have paid them? They have built splendid churches at Rome, and bought rich dresses for the Pope and Cardinals to wear, and gilded coaches for them to ride in They have built, and are building, expensive colleges and schools, to instruct the children of rich *Protestants*, hoping to make Catholic Priests of them Meanwhile, your children, and your father's children, and your grandfather's children, and your other ancestors, have been left to get a little learning as you could or grow up in ignorance.

Is not this all true? Only think how much money you have paid them yourselves Do you know what they have done with it? When a Protestant has given a man a dollar for some religious purpose, he must show what he has done with it, or he will never get another. Is it so with you? Do you know what your Priests do with all the money they receive from you? Have not you and your Catholic neighbors paid them so much, that they might have taught you, and your neighbors, and your children, to read? If you and your ancestors, for five hundred years past or two hundred years past, had been Protestants, you would have been taught.

Now, my friends, think, a little while, whether Priests who have so shamefully neglected their duty are worthy of your confidence You and your fathers have tried them for hundreds of years Have you not tried them long enough? Is it not time for you to say your children shall be taught to read? Is it not time for you to choose such schools for them as you find to be best? This is a free country. The Priests have no right to control you in the education of your children.

Some of you do send your children to our public schools. The teachers tell me that they behave as well, and learn as fast, as any children under their care I am glad to hear it. Your children, thus educated, will be intelligent and respectable. Some of them will be among our great men in another generation. If the Priests will furnish schools for your children which are as good as the public schools, you have a perfect right to send your children to which you please. But see to it that they go to good schools,—schools where they learn well. If you are determined to send them to such schools, probably the Priests will not object, for they know they cannot help themselves. Perhaps they will even encourage you. But whether they do or not, see to it that your children are well educated.

Your Priests tell you, that the Roman Catholic Church is infallible. Suppose it is so How do you know what that church teaches? Some three weeks ago a part of the doings of the Council of Trent, sanctioned by the Pope's Bull, were published. It was copied from a book published by Roman Catholics, and sanctioned by the Roman Catholic authorities in church and state. Yet the Catholic Sentinel calls it a "Protestant slander." Now, if such documents, so published, are not to be depended upon, how are we to know, or how can you know, what the Roman Catholic Church really teaches? Especially, how do those of you who cannot read know what the church teaches?

Do you say, that your Priests tell you what the church teaches? How do you know that they tell you truly? How do you know that they do not deceive you? How do you know that the Priests themselves know what the doctrines of the church are? Do you believe that every Priest is infallible? Martin Luther was once a Roman Catholic Priest Was he infallible? Calvin, too, was once a Roman Catholic Priest. Was he infallible? Mr. Samuel B Smith, who is now publishing a newspaper, called "The Downfall of Babylon," was a Roman Catholic Priest only some two years ago. Was he infallible? If they were infallible, then they did right to leave the Roman Catholic Church.

But you may be told, that these men were apostates—they left the church, and became Protestants. True, they became Protestants. But if the Roman Catholic Church had been right, and they when Priests had been infallible, they could not have left it. And then, think of Archbishop Penolon. He did not leave the church. Yet he published a book, which the Pope condemned, and he confessed that it contained erroneous doctrines. Was he infallible when he wrote that book? And was the Pope infallible when he condemned it? And was Fenelon still infallible when he joined the Pope in condemning it?

No, your Priests are not infallible. They may mistake. How do you know that those of them who teach you do not mistake? How do you know that what they teach is the true doctrine of the church? How can you know, unless you read the Bible for yourselves, and find that the Bible teaches the same doctrines?

Do your Priests ever tell you to pray to the Virgin Mary, the mother of our Lord Jesus Christ? I suppose they do You know whether they tell you so or not. How do you know that this is a doctrine of the true Catholic Church? Do you say, that all Catholics practise it? You mean, all Catholics *with whom you are acquainted.* Perhaps there are other Catholics who do not pray to her How do you know? Do your Priests tell you? How do your Priests know? And how do you know that they tell the truth?

I suppose that all Roman Catholics do pray to the Virgin Mary; though I do not see how either you or I can know it infallibly. But I suppose that you pray to her here in Boston, and some of your friends pray to her in New York, and others in Pennsylvania, and others in Ohio, and others in Ireland, all at once. Now stop and think for a moment;—can she hear you all at once? When you pray to God, he can hear you, because he is an infinite Spirit, and is everywhere at the same time; but Mary is not God. She is not everywhere at the same time. She cannot listen at once to a million of people, some here, and some three thousand, and some ten thousand miles off. When several people speak to you at once, you cannot listen to them all, and understand them all. And do you believe that Mary can listen to a million, who are all speaking at once, in different parts of the world, so as to know what they all say? Do you say the infallible church teaches that she can hear them all? How do you know that the church teaches it? How do you know that your Priests tell the truth when they say the church teaches it? And how do you know that the church is infallible? You have only the word of the Priests for it, and perhaps they mistake. And if the true church is infallible, how do you know that the Church of Rome is the true church? The Priests tell you so; but they may be wrong And besides, do you not see that Mary *cannot* listen to a million of prayers at once, so as to understand them all? Do you not see that this must be an error? Do you not see that, if the Church of Rome teaches this, it teaches what is not true?

If your Priests teach you to pray to Mary, they teach you wrong God says, that "whoever shall call upon the name of the Lord shall be saved" Romans x 13. He does not say that whoever shall call on the name of *Mary* shall be saved. God teaches one thing, and your Priests teach another

I must say a few words to you about *images.* In the second of the ten commandments, God says, "Thou shalt not bow down unto them." Do you bow down unto them? If you do, you disobey God. If your Priests teach you to bow down unto them, they teach you to break God's commandment.

I could quote to you what Roman Catholic councils have decreed, and what Popes have said on this subject; for I can read Latin as well as your Priests But when I quote what Popes and councils say, the Sentinel calls it "Protestant slander." Your infallible church has no infallible books, in which any one can infallibly learn its doctrines; at least, I cannot find any, which your Priests and editors will allow to be infallible. But no matter. I am writing to you, and you know whether they teach you to bow down to images or not. If they do, they teach you to do wickedly; and if you follow such teaching, you offend God.

Perhaps the Priests will tell you, that you do not worship the image, but only worship God by means of the image. But take notice, God says, "Thou shalt not *bow down* unto them." Now, suppose you bow down unto an image for the purpose of worshipping God; still you break God's commandment; for he says, "Thou shalt not bow down unto them" When God tells you that you must not do a thing, he never sends Priests to tell you that you *must* do it. If any Priest tells you to bow down before an image, you must know by that that God did not send him. I have been told that Bishop Cheverus some years ago said, in one of his sermons, that you must have images, because you are so ignorant that you cannot worship without them; and I have read the words of some Popes and Bishops who speak in the same way. But is this true? Did not God know whether you ought to have images or not, when he said, "Thou shalt not bow down unto them?"

But can you not think of God when you do not see an image? You know that you can. You can remember how kind he has been to you, in preserving your lives; in giving you food to eat, and raiment to put on; and in giving his Son to die for you, that your sins may be pardoned. You can feel thankful to him for all his goodness. You can say, heartily, "O God, I thank thee for all thy goodness to me" You can wish him to continue to take care of you, and supply your wants, and forgive your sins, and help you to keep his commandments. You can think of God, and ask him to do all these things, without having an image to look at. You know you can. Do it, and that will be worshipping God without the use of an image. You know you can do it. You are not such great dunces as your Priests and Bishops pretend to think you are. You can worship God without an image; and you can learn to worship him still better than you now can.

Perhaps some of your Priests will tell you, that God has given no such commandment in respect to images. In some of their books, in which they pretend to give the whole of the ten commandments, they have left out the second, and divided the tenth into two, so as to make out the number. When the Protestants found it out, and told the public of it, the Priests had other editions of the same books published, with all the commandments in them, as they should be. These they show, to prove that the story about their leaving out the second commandment is a "Protestant slander." Books of both kinds are still in circulation. I do not know which you have, or which your Catholic neighbors have. I mention it, that you may not be deceived if you happen to have one of the false books, or if you have a false Priest, who tells you there is no such commandment.

Think seriously of these things. Remember God's commandment, which forbids you to bow down before images. Worship him in your minds, by thinking of him and expressing your thoughts. Speak to him. Thank him for his goodness, and ask him for what you need. He will understand you. If you mean honestly, he will know it, and will be pleased with your worship.

You know whether your Priests tell you any thing about *purgatory*. You know whether you ever gave them any money to pray, or say mass, for the souls of your friends, who, you supposed, might be in purgatory. You know whether you ever gave them any money to pray or say mass for your own souls, when you are dead. You know, too, whether they ever told you to give money for such purposes. You know about these things. I do not; but I suppose they teach you that there is such a place as purgatory.

Now, how do they know that there is any such place? How did they find it out? There is not one word about it in the whole Bible. God, in the Bible, has not told them that there is any such place. How, then, do they know that there is any purgatory? Do they say, the church has decided it? How do you know that the church has decided it? How do you know that it was not some false Pope, or some wicked, heretical council, that made that decision? Do the Priests tell you? The Priests are not infallible. Perhaps they mistake. But if the church did make such a decision, how did the church know? God did not tell them. We have all God's word in the Bible, and it says not one word about purgatory.

How, then, do the Priests know that there is a purgatory? Have any of them ever been there? No. Did they ever see any body that had been there? I think they will not pretend that they have. The truth is, that there is no such place.

Do you ask me why they tell such a story? You have a better opportunity to know than I have. You know whether they get any of your money by telling it. If they do, it may be that they tell it for the sake of getting your money. What would you think of any body else who should get away your money by telling you what is not true?

I do not mean to say that all your Priests *know* that there is no such place as purgatory. Perhaps some of them believe it; for some of them are very ignorant. After all the noise they make about their learning, some of them have only a little Latin, which they have learned by heart without understanding it, and cannot read a word of Greek or Hebrew. But if such ignorant Priests do believe it, that does not make it true. Our Savior tells you not to follow such blind guides, lest you both fall into the ditch

Perhaps you say you are a sinner, and unfit for heaven; and ask what you shall do, if there is no purgatory, where you can suffer what you deserve, unless the Priest procures your release by saying mass for you. I will tell you. Go into your closet. Go into any place where you can be alone. There think of Christ. Remember the words of the holy Apostle, written in the Holy Scriptures, "the blood of Christ cleanseth from all sin." Think of Christ, who died for your sins Believe that God is there, and can hear you. Think of your sins. Confess them, honestly, to God. Ask him to forgive you, for Christ's sake. Do not pray to Mary, or some other Saint Do not ask any of them to intercede with God for you. Speak to God yourself Tell him that you are a sinner. Tell him all the truth about yourself. Ask him to forgive your sins. Believe that he is ready and willing to hear your prayer, and to forgive your sins, for the sake of his Son, who died to redeem you. If you really feel sorry that you have sinned, and truly wish to serve God hereafter, he will accept and pardon you. Do not be afraid to speak to your heavenly Father. He loved you so much as to give his Son to die for you; and will he not be pleased to hear your prayer and forgive your sins? Certainly he will. Go to him. Confess your sins to him. Ask pardon of him. He will forgive you. He will give you his Spirit, to lead you in the right way. When you die, he will not send you to hell, for you are pardoned; nor to purgatory, for there is no such place; but will take you to heaven at once.

280·20 REE

CPSIA information can be obtained
at www.ICGtesting.com
Printed in the USA
LVOW01s1742170616
493067LV00025B/635/P

9 781331 75196